Toward the End of Growth

CHARLES F. WESTOFF

is Associate Director of the Office of
Population Research and Professor of Sociology
at Princeton University and former executive
director of the Commission on Population Growth
and the American Future. He is the co-author
of *Reproduction in the United States: 1965*
and *From Now to Zero: Fertility,
Contraception and Abortion in the U.S.*

CHARLES F. WESTOFF and others

Toward the End of Growth

POPULATION IN AMERICA

A SPECTRUM BOOK

PRENTICE-HALL, INC. • ENGLEWOOD CLIFFS, NEW JERSEY

Library of Congress Cataloging in Publication Data
MAIN ENTRY UNDER TITLE:

Toward the end of growth.

(A Spectrum Book)
Outgrowth of a conference held in Buck Hill Falls, Pa.,
Sept. 6–7, 1972.
Includes bibliographies.
1. United States—Population. 2. Birth control—
United States. I. Westoff, Charles F. [DNLM:
1. Family planning—U.S.—Congresses. 2. Population
growth—U.S.—Congresses. HQ766.5.U5 T737 1972]
HB3505.T68   301.32′9′73   73–7849
ISBN 0–13–925792–6
ISBN 0–13–925784–5 (pbk.)

PRENTICE-HALL INTERNATIONAL, INC. (*London*)
PRENTICE-HALL OF AUSTRALIA PTY., LTD. (*Sydney*)
PRENTICE-HALL OF CANADA, LTD. (*Toronto*)
PRENTICE-HALL OF INDIA PRIVATE LIMITED (*New Delhi*)
PRENTICE-HALL OF JAPAN, INC. (*Tokyo*)

Contents

Preface

The origin of this volume can be traced back to the interest of the Ortho Pharmaceutical Corporation in sponsoring a conference on United States population and population-policy developments. This conference was held in Buck Hill Falls, Pennsylvania, September 6 and 7, 1972.

Some of the work reflected in this book—particularly that on the various consequences of growth and the population projection material—was originally undertaken as research for the Commission on Population Growth and the American Future and is summarized only briefly here. The fuller accounts can be found in the final report of the Commission and in its background research reports. Other papers draw heavily on the 1965 and 1970 National Fertility Studies conducted at Princeton University by Norman Ryder and myself, supported by the Center for Population Research of the National Institute of Child Health and Human Development.

I would like to acknowledge with special thanks the editorial work of Patricia Taylor, of the Office of Population Research at Princeton University, and I want to express again my appreciation to the Ortho people for making possible a very stimulating meeting and, I hope, a useful publication.

Toward the End of Growth

CHARLES F. WESTOFF ═══════════════════════════

1. Introduction

Only a few years ago there was a great concern in this country about the rapid increase of population. Public officials suddenly became aware that the nation's population might reach 300 million by the end of the century. Environmentalists were sounding the alarm that continued population growth spelled disaster. A new organization was formed to promote the cause of Zero Population Growth. And in 1970 a Commission on Population Growth and the American Future was created by Congress at the request of President Nixon, who, in July 1969, warned that:

> One of the most serious challenges to human destiny in the last third of this century will be the growth of population. Whether man's response to that challenge will be a cause for pride or for despair in the year 2000 will depend very much on what we do today.

Today these concerns seem almost dated. The Bureau of the Census has published downward revisions of the number of people expected by the end of the century. The birthrate, despite most predictions to the contrary, keeps sinking lower and lower. The familiar terms "population explosion" and "baby boom" have been replaced by phrases like "birth dearth" and "baby bust." In some quarters of the Western world that are experiencing the same phenomenon, people are expressing concern about the end of population growth and the possibilities of future declines in numbers. When the U.S. Population Commission issued its final report, the president received it with little evident enthusiasm and rejected two of its more controversial recommendations. Even in light of the dizzying rate of change that is typical of modern America, this overnight shift from crisis to complacency is difficult to comprehend.

What could account for such a drastic change? Was there never a crisis to begin with or was it simply perceived late? Is America now back on the road to zero population growth or are we just resting before embarking on a second round of the baby boom, the so-called "echo effect" of the post–World War II baby boom? Does it really make any difference whether we average two or three children?

This book is an effort to answer some of these questions. It begins with reports on some of the current research dealing with patterns of fertility control in contemporary America. Logically, we start in Chapter 2 with unmarried young people. Melvin Zelnik and John F. Kantner have undertaken the first and only reliable large-scale study of the sexual and contraceptive habits of teenage girls in America. They have addressed themselves to such questions as: How frequently do unmarried teenagers have sexual intercourse? With how many partners? How much do they know about the biology of conception? How often do they use contraception? What methods of contraception do teenage girls most commonly use? Data from their study reveal little regular contraceptive practice and great ignorance of the biology of conception.

The decline of the birthrate in America has been greatly facilitated by the modernization of contraceptive practice among married couples. Recent changes in patterns of contraceptive use are described in Chapter 3. The fact that the pill has now become the most popular method used, coupled with a dramatic increase in the use of the IUD and a greater reliance on surgical sterilization, has greatly enhanced the ability of American couples to control their fertility. This veritable revolution in contraceptive practice has undoubtedly been responsible for the decline we have seen in the rate of unwanted fertility, which in turn has played a major role in the overall decline in the birthrate. Whites and blacks, Catholics and non-Catholics have all been affected. In fact, there has been virtually a mass defection of Catholics from the traditional teachings of the Church on birth control.

The increasing acceptance of sterilization and abortion in the U.S. is described in Chapter 4 by Larry L. Bumpass and Harriet B. Presser. Attitudes toward both procedures have grown more favorable in the last few years, to the point where vasectomies have almost become fashionable in some quarters. The statistics on abortion in New York bear eloquent testimony to the inadequacy of even today's improved contraceptives. What is the trend in attitudes toward abortion? What kind of women are having abortions in New York? Their characteristics and the demographic significance of the increased practice of both sterilization and abortion are reviewed.

The first section concludes with an analysis by S. Bruce Shearer of probable future developments in contraceptive technology. These prospects include new generations of IUDs, low dose orals, postcoital approaches, a male pill, and new techniques of sterilization. Shearer concludes that such new developments will offer a significant but marginal improvement over existing methods but that the perfect contraceptive, although feasible, is not yet visible on the horizon.

The extent of fertility control and the attitudes of couples toward having children will have a great effect on the future rate of population growth. In Chapter 6, Norman B. Ryder examines recent trends in American fertility and the contraction of racial, religious, and educational differences. The probable causes of the decline in fertility are enumerated.

With all of the current speculation about the causes of the decline in the birthrate, little attention has been paid to the fact that in historical perspective it can be viewed simply as the resumption of a long-term trend. This is brought into clear focus in Chapter 7 by Michael S. Teitelbaum, who shows that there is very little that is unique in the American experience, with the possible exception of the fact that the baby boom lasted longer here than elsewhere. Teitelbaum's review of the patterns of population growth in other countries of the developed world indicates how common is the resumption of the trend toward zero population growth.

What do all of these developments imply for future population growth in this country? In Chapter 8, Norman B. Ryder leads us through the calculation of a population projection that combines both optimal and likely demographic features: fertility falls to the replacement level soon, the average age of reproduction rises appreciably, the annual number of births stabilizes, and the population ultimately stops growing just short of 300 million. Only the plausibility of such projections can be judged. Their accuracy will have to be assessed in retrospect.

Having sketched the developments in fertility regulation, examined trends in fertility, and looked into population growth in the future, we turn in the third section of the book to the "so what" question: what difference does it make if we grow faster or slower or not at all? In Chapter 9, Stephen Enke examines the effects of population growth on the national economy and on different types of industry. Enke assesses the implications of declining fertility for the size of the labor force, savings and output per worker, and per capita income. Although he finds that some types of industry would benefit more than others from slower population growth, the time available to adjust to population change is sufficient to avoid serious problems. Enke's conclusion is that the national economy would benefit more from an earlier attainment of population stabilization than from a later one.

One of the most emotionally charged segments of the population debate concerns the effects of population growth on the environment. One extreme argues that population growth multiplies the impact of wealth and technology on the environment and is therefore a major culprit. The opposite extreme maintains that environmental deterioration has resulted mainly from certain kinds of technology and that population growth is not implicated. In Chapter 10, Ronald Ridker introduces the results of research designed to isolate the effects of U.S. population growth on the use of resources and on the environment. Prudence and caution, rather than crisis and alarm, characterize his conclusions.

Will population growth have any effect on government services? In Chapter 11, Robert Parke traces the implications of alternative rates of growth for federal government expenditures on education, health, and welfare. He concludes that considerable gains could be realized from slower growth, only in the case of education. Parke goes on to examine the significance of continued growth for our national security, for the size of congressional constituencies, for the system of representative government, and for the administration of justice. One of the inevitable consequences of the slowing and eventual stabilization of population growth is the fact that the proportion of older people in the population will increase. Parke discusses some of the social implications of this change.

In Chapter 12, Harriet B. Presser shifts the analysis of the impacts of population growth to the level of the individual woman and the family and explores the consequences of perfect fertility control. If no births occurred before they were wanted, and if family size were smaller, what would be the effects on the roles of women in society and on the future of the family? Presser describes several probable consequences and presents the case that control over the timing of the first birth would be the most critical change.

How have national governments reacted to these demographic developments and their likely impacts? Have the modern nations of the world come to grips with the population question and formulated population policies? A review of population policies in 15 developed countries is presented by Bernard Berelson in Chapter 13. Their demographic situations are described and the national and official groups concerned with population policy are identified. Many of the countries have appointed population commissions of one sort or another, testifying to the emerging interest in population questions. The legal policies of each country on contraception, abortion, and related services are catalogued, as are the availability of family assistance programs, the courses of action followed on international migration, and the participation of women in the labor force.

The concluding chapter traces recent developments in U.S. population policy. The results of a recent opinion poll are used to summarize the attitudes of the public toward population growth, population policy, and related topics. The views of the environmental movement, the business community, the Catholic Church, ethnic groups, and the women's liberation movement are described. Chapter 14 also traces the history of government attitudes toward population and describes the recent report of the Commission on Population Growth and the American Future and some of the reactions to it. The chapter then concludes that the United States does not yet have an explicit population policy and that such a policy is unlikely to emerge until the behavior of individuals and the welfare of society become regarded as more widely divergent than they are today.

MELVIN ZELNIK **/** *JOHN F. KANTNER* ═══════════

2. Sex and Contraception among Unmarried Teenagers

Premarital sexual intercourse, especially among females, is the subject of a great deal of controversy in the United States. Both scholars and journalists debate at length whether or not we are experiencing a sexual revolution. Put more prosaically, these writers seem to be asking if premarital intercourse occurs more frequently or less frequently today than it did in the past. Unfortunately, most of the arguments seem to be based less on fact than on intuition or sentiment, for we have very little evidence that bears directly on the question.

We know virtually nothing about the premarital sexual activities of those who were teenagers one or two generations ago, and it is not likely that we shall ever know more. Kinsey's well-known data on sexuality were based largely on the recollections of older women who did not constitute a statistically acceptable sample of the whole population.

Melvin Zelnik is a Ford Foundation Population Consultant to the National Institute for Public Health (Demographic Division) in Indonesia. He is on leave from Johns Hopkins University, where he is a professor of population dynamics in the School of Public Health.

John F. Kantner is a professor of population dynamics in the School of Public Health at Johns Hopkins University. A specialist in fertility, he has served on the staff of the Population Council and was formerly a professor of sociology at Western Ontario University.

Their research is supported by a grant from the National Institute of Child Health and Human Development.

Other findings have come from highly selective studies of clinical populations or from studies of college students in one or another introductory social science course, neither of which is representative of teenagers in general.

In this chapter, we report on data obtained in a field survey conducted during mid-1971 (Zelnik & Kantner, 1972). Interviews were completed with a representative sample of 4,611 females, aged 15 to 19, living in households and college dormitories in the United States (excluding Alaska and Hawaii). To ensure a sufficient number of interviews with black females, a sampling scheme stratified by race was employed. As a result, there were 1,479 interviews with black females and 3,132 interviews with whites and other races.* In order to provide national estimates, the sample was inflated to produce agreement with the counts, by age and race, of the 1970 Census of Population.

The sample includes females who have had intercourse as well as those who have not, females who have used contraceptives as well as those who have not, females who have been pregnant as well as those who have not, and females who have been married as well as those who have not. In this chapter, we will restrict our comments largely to females who had never been married at the time of the survey. This group which accounts for about 90 percent of the sample, represents a significant and identifiable segment of the population, about whom it would be useful to know more. Although our data do not reveal what changes are taking place in premarital sexual activities, they do provide a necessary base for understanding the present situation and for measuring any future change. It should be pointed out that at least 57 percent of the females who were or had been married had premarital intercourse. Thus, in talking about the sexual activities of those who had never been married, we are presenting a slightly biased description of the premarital sexual activity of all the females in our study. The omission of the ever-married also should be kept in mind when we are considering differences, by age and race, in the various facets of sexual behavior.

Our data indicate that slightly over one-quarter of the never-married females have had intercourse (see Table 2-1). As one would expect, the proportion increases with age, from 14 percent at age 15 to 46 percent at age 19. There is a substantial difference between blacks and whites at each age. For example, at age 15, about 11 percent of the whites and about 32 percent of the blacks have had intercourse; at 19, 40 percent of the whites and 81 percent of the blacks have had

---

* To simplify the presentation, we will refer to this latter group—whites and other races—simply as whites.

TABLE 2–1. NEVER-MARRIED FEMALES
WHO HAVE HAD INTERCOURSE
(BY AGE AND RACE)

Age		Black	White	Total
15		32.3%	10.8%	13.8%
16		46.4	17.5	21.2
17		57.0	21.7	26.6
18		60.4	33.5	37.1
19		80.8	40.4	46.1
	Total	53.6%	23.4%	27.6%

intercourse. Combining all age groups the proportion of blacks who have had intercourse is slightly more than double the proportion of whites who have had intercourse.

The survey also attempted to determine how knowledgeable these young women are—both those who have and those who have not had intercourse—about the age when they are first able to conceive, the period during the menstrual cycle when pregnancy can occur, and the various methods of contraception. We might expect the sexually active females to be more knowledgeable, but the data do not consistently support this view. With reference to the first question, for example, there appears to be only a small difference in knowledge between those who have had intercourse and those who have not. More than half of each group believe that a girl can become pregnant at menarche that is, as soon as she begins to menstruate. Oddly enough, the proportion holding this erroneous belief increases with age (see Table 2-2). A somewhat higher proportion of blacks are correct in their assessment that there is a delay between menarche and the onset of fecundity. This assessment, correct though it is, may be part of the reason why blacks tend to defer the use of contraception more than whites.

Knowledge about the period of risk during the menstrual cycle is also limited and shows rather sharp differences between the races. Fewer than 20 percent of all black females, compared with over 40 percent of all white females, are aware that the time of risk occurs about two weeks after the beginning of menstruation. Almost 50 percent of the blacks and about 41 percent of the whites see the time of greatest risk occurring either right before, right after, or during the menses. The remaining 34 percent of blacks and 15 percent of whites

TABLE 2–2.   CORRECT RESPONSES OF NEVER-MARRIED FEMALES
TO QUESTIONS ABOUT ONSET OF FECUNDITY AND
PERIOD OF GREATEST RISK DURING THE
MENSTRUAL CYCLE (BY AGE AND RACE)

Age	Onset of Fecundity			Period of Risk		
	Black	White	Total	Black	White	Total
15	48.1%	45.9%	46.2%	17.1%	30.4%	28.5%
16	44.5	40.7	41.2	16.9	36.4	33.9
17	40.4	32.9	33.9	17.8	41.9	38.5
18	42.9	30.2	31.9	16.7	52.9	48.0
19	28.4	31.4	30.9	22.4	56.2	51.4
Total	41.5%	36.9%	37.5%	18.0%	42.4%	39.0%

hold the view that pregnancy can occur at any time during the menstrual cycle.

Having had premarital sex does not appear to affect the knowledge of black females about the time of greatest risk. Among whites,
however, 54 percent of those who have had intercourse can correctly
identify the time of greatest risk, while only 40 percent of those who
have not engaged in sexual relations can do so. In addition, whites
show an increase with age in the proportion identifying the correct
time of risk regardless of whether they have had intercourse, whereas
blacks do not.

With regard to pregnancy prevention, how important it is for a
girl to understand the menstrual cycle properly depends partly on what
type of contraception, if any, she is using. The more closely a method
is linked to each sexual encounter, the greater is the likelihood that
those who hold erroneous beliefs will experience an unplanned pregnancy. Reducing the substantial ignorance we encountered among
young women would undoubtedly enhance the effectiveness of whatever contraceptive methods they are now using. The extent to which
young women are misinformed on these matters is surprising in view
of the attention given to sex education in recent years. Very few of
our respondents answer "don't know" to questions about the onset of
fecundity or the period of risk during the menstrual cycle. Effective
sex education, therefore, would seem to depend as much on countering
false notions as on providing new information.

Virtually all females report having heard of at least one of the following eight contraceptive methods: the pill, foam, intrauterine device (IUD), diaphragm, condom, douche, rhythm, or withdrawal. Even among the least knowledgeable group—blacks who have not had intercourse—only about 3 percent have not heard of any of the eight, while 43 percent have heard of six or more of the methods. Among the most knowledgeable group—whites who have had intercourse—all report having heard of at least one method and about 84 percent have heard of six or more.

The most commonly known method is oral contraception. Almost all—98 percent—of all females report knowledge of the pill. The second most commonly known method is the condom, with 86 percent reporting knowledge of it. At the opposite extreme, only about 50 percent report having heard of the IUD. Knowledge about the pill and the condom, is uniformly high, but knowledge of the other six methods increases with age, is higher among those who have had intercourse than among those who have not, and tends to be higher among whites than among blacks. The overwhelming majority of these young women believe that responsibility for use of contraception should be shared jointly by the male and female partners rather than allocated to either the male or the female alone. It is not entirely clear, however, what "joint responsibility" means in practical terms. In this context it could well be an expression of how an ideal relationship should handle this problem. In group discussions which were organized to discuss this and similar matters the views that men were uncooperative regarding contraception was heard frequently.

Let us turn now to those females who have had intercourse and ask how frequently they engage in such activity. Judging from responses to a question on the frequency of intercourse during the month prior to being interviewed, the answer is "not very often." The most common response given was zero times. There is some increase in frequency with age, and slightly higher frequencies are found among whites than among blacks.

What about promiscuity? Again, taking a time span of one month, there appears to be little of it. Among those who report having had intercourse at least once during the previous month, 90 percent have had one partner. Since relatively few have had intercourse more than one or two times during the previous month, the opportunity for a high degree of promiscuity does not exist. When we consider data on the number of partners involved since first having intercourse, we find that about 60 percent of both whites and blacks have had only one partner. As we would expect the number of partners increases with age, and this relationship is somewhat more pronounced among whites than among blacks. These data on frequency of intercourse and number of partners fail to support the widespread notion that blacks tend to engage in intercourse frequently and with a number of partners. In fact, although proportionately more blacks than whites have had intercourse, it appears that whites have sex more frequently and are somewhat more promiscuous.

Most young women who have had intercourse have used contraception at some time. Only about 15 percent of each race report never having used contraception. The proportion who have never used any method is highest among the 15-year-olds, decreases at ages 16 and 17, and then levels off.

The bulk of those using contraception use it "sometimes," rather than "always." That is, they report that they have had unprotected intercourse at some time. About 63 percent of all sexually active females, or three-quarters of all who have ever used contraception, rely on it only "sometimes." The remainder, except for a small number who gave no answer to the question, are "always" users. A slightly higher proportion of whites than blacks are "always" users and a slightly higher proportion of blacks than whites are "sometimes" users. At any age, and for both racial groups, those who have never used contraception plus those who have sometimes failed to use it constitute a solid majority. Clearly, there is a high degree of chance taking among sexually active unmarried teenagers.

The extent of this risk taking is illustrated by the low proportion of women who used a contraceptive the last time they had intercourse. About 50 percent of all sexually active females report that their last sexual act was unprotected (see Table 2-3). Here again there are substantial differences by age. Only about 30 percent of the 15-year-olds were protected, whereas about 63 percent of the 19-year-olds used contraception. At age 19, differences between blacks and whites are relatively small. The relation of age to contraceptive use is even more striking if we restrict our attention to those using contraception "sometimes." Of this group, only about 23 percent of those aged 15 used contraception the last time they had intercourse, while about 61 percent of those aged 19 did so. Again, differences between blacks and whites are small.

These data on contraceptive use reveal a number of important points. The proportion of females who have used contraception is considerably below the proportion who know of at least one method of contraception. Secondly, the proportion who used contraception the last time they had intercourse is below the proportion who have ever used contraception. Both points hold, regardless of age or race. Third, even among the users of contraception, the younger the female, the more likely she is to have never used contraception and the less likely she is

TABLE 2-3.   USE OF CONTRACEPTION AT TIME OF LAST
              INTERCOURSE

Age	All Sexually Active[a],[b]			"Sometimes" Users		
	Black	White	Total	Black	White	Total
15	31.8%	29.9%	30.5%	21.2%	23.2%	22.5%
16	38.2	41.2	40.3	35.9	32.1	33.2
17	46.4	46.5	46.5	37.9	42.7	41.3
18	52.5	54.0	53.7	49.2	52.4	51.7
19	55.4	65.1	62.8	58.2	62.6	61.3
Total	46.4%	50.9%	49.7%	44.3%	47.6%	46.7%

[a]Excludes approximately 5 percent who gave no answer to the question, plus those who gave no answer at all relative to contraceptive use.

[b]Includes those who "always," "sometimes," and "never" used contraception.

to have used contraception the last time she had intercourse. And last, differences between blacks and whites in use of contraception are small.

What methods of contraception do these young women use? The majority, 69 percent, have used only one or two methods. Slightly more report use of one method than two. Use of three or more methods is slightly higher among blacks than among whites—36 and 29 percent, respectively. The most widely used method among blacks is the condom, which has been used by about 57 percent of all sexually active black females. The second and third most popular methods among blacks are the douche, 43 percent, and withdrawal, 38 percent. Among whites, the three most widely used methods are withdrawal, 59 percent, the condom, 48 percent, and the pill, 23 percent. Of course, these figures refer to all sexually active females. They would be higher if we restricted our attention to those who have used contraception. Interestingly enough, the most popular method among blacks, the condom, and the most popular method among whites, withdrawal, are both thought of as "male" methods.

The ranking of the method used most recently is similar to that for methods ever used. The similarity does not, however, hold in each age group. The three methods most recently used by blacks, which account for about 80 percent of total use, are the condom either alone or in combination with another method, the pill, and the douche. About 42 percent reported use of the condom, 26 percent the pill, and 12 percent the douche (see Table 2-4). Among whites, the three leading

TABLE 2–4. MOST RECENTLY USED CONTRACEPTIVE
METHOD (BY RACE)

Method	Black	White	Total
Pill	26.5%	25.0%	25.5%
Foam	3.5	2.7	2.9
IUD	3.6	0.6	1.4
Diaphragm	1.2	1.7	1.5
Condom[a]	41.8	29.3	32.6
Douche	12.1	2.9	5.3
Withdrawal	8.5	33.0	26.5
Douche and withdrawal combined	2.3	2.2	2.3
Rhythm	0.5	2.6	2.0
All methods	100.0%	100.0%	100.0%

[a] Alone or in combination.

methods are withdrawal, the condom, and the pill. These three methods account for 87 percent of total most recent use; withdrawal represents 33 percent, the condom 29 percent, and the pill 25 percent.

Although the proportions reporting use of the IUD are low, especially among whites, this and the pill are the only methods that show consistent increases in use with age. The other methods either decline with age or show no relationship to age. A greater proportion of blacks than whites report use of the IUD at each age. For the pill, whites exceed blacks only at age 19, with 43 percent of the 19-year-old whites reporting recent use of the pill in contrast to 33 percent of the 19-year-old blacks. These differences are probably a reflection of the greater extent to which organized contraceptive programs are reaching blacks, especially young blacks. In general differences between blacks and whites in the choice of methods may be influenced also by differences in the average age at which sex and contraception begin, since the data suggest that methods such as withdrawal and the condom are abandoned for methods such as oral contraception the longer contraception is practised.

Those who sometimes used contraception were asked, in effect, why they did not always use contraception. The reasons given do not refer to any particular occasion. Each respondent was allowed to give several reasons. The discussion here is based on the first reason given by each girl. There are marked differences between blacks and whites in the reasons for not using contraception. Proportionately, twice as many blacks as whites (24 percent versus 12 percent) either wanted to become pregnant or were unconcerned if that were the result. About an equal number of blacks fall into each category. Among whites, one-third were trying to become pregnant and two-thirds did not mind if that occurred.

However, the single most important reason given is the respondents' belief that they could not become pregnant. This was the reason given by about 49 percent of blacks and 59 percent of whites. Blacks tended to feel they were infecund in some general sense—that they were too young, or not exposed often enough. Whites were more inclined to play the menstrual cycle for protection. Such reasons account for about two-thirds of all nonuse. The remaining responses cluster around questions of logistics ("contraception not available," "didn't know where to obtain"), hedonism ("no fun to use," "too inconvenient"), and assorted objections ("dangerous," "wrong to use"). Among these, the most important is that contraception was not available at the time it was needed; this was reported by about 10 percent of blacks and 12 percent of whites. Thus, the data on reasons for not using contraception seem to suggest that making inexpensive contraception readily available to sexually active unwed teenagers will have a considerably smaller impact on teenage illegitimacy than is often claimed. It may of course make a difference in the type of method used. For example the progression from reliance on withdrawal and condom to the use of orals that is associated with age may be to a greater or lesser extent a matter of increased access to professional sources of contraception.

This paper has been concerned with various facets of sexual behavior among unmarried teenagers aged 15 to 19 in the United States. Not surprisingly, sexual activity increases with age among this group. Proportionately more blacks than whites have had intercourse. However, racial differences in frequency of intercourse are negligible, although frequency tends to increase with age. Most of the sexually active girls did not have intercourse in the month preceding the interview, and most of the sexually active have had intercourse with only one partner. Although there are exceptions, the picture is not one of rampant sexual activity among the sexually experienced.

Many teenagers today are poorly informed as to when the possibility of pregnancy first begins and what are the periods of greatest and least risk during the menstrual cycle. Whites are somewhat better informed about the menstrual cycle and become better informed as they become older or as they become sexually more experienced. The level of knowledge among blacks does not improve much either with age or sexual experience.

Limiting the discussion to unmarried females has caused us to ignore two important areas of behavior—age at first intercourse, and the relation of this age to the age at first use of contraception. Proper treatment of these two questions would necessarily require the inclusion of ever-married females who had intercourse before marriage. Preliminary results, based on an analysis of all premarital sexual behavior, do not alter the finding that proportionately more blacks than whites engage in premarital intercourse, at least in the age range under consideration. In addition (and this we believe to be another important difference between blacks and whites), blacks have their initial sexual experience at an earlier age than whites.

These results indicate also that the later the age of initial sexual activity, the more likely that contraceptive use begins at the same age. However, at each age of first intercourse, proportionately more whites than blacks start to use contraception at that age. The relatively greater deferment of contraceptive use after the onset of sexuality is a major difference between blacks and whites in contraceptive behavior.

Finally, combining the experience of both married and never-married women makes it possible for us to estimate the probability of first premarital intercourse by age. For never-married females, the first instance of intercourse would obviously be a case of premarital intercourse. In order to determine whether the first intercourse of women who have been married occurred premaritally, it is necessary to compare their age at first intercourse with their age at marriage. When the age at the two events differs it is easy to determine whether or not the first intercourse occurred before or after marriage. Where the age is the same, the problem is more complicated and involves making minimum and maximum estimates of the probability of first intercourse by assuming in the maximum case that all such instances of first intercourse occurred premaritally and in the minimum case that none did. For a discussion of the procedures used in estimating first intercourse probabilities, see Zelnik, Melvin, & John F. Kantner, "The Probability of Premarital Intercourse," *Social Science Research,* 3 (September 1972). It is then possible to classify each first premarital intercourse by the woman's age at the time it occurred and to compute the probability of first premarital intercourse at each age. Minimum estimates constructed in this manner are shown in Table 2-5. For example, by reading across the second row we can learn that a black female

TABLE 2-5. MINIMUM ESTIMATES OF THE
INDEPENDENT PROBABILITY OF
FIRST PREMARITAL INTERCOURSE
(BY AGE AND RACE)

Age at First Premarital Intercourse	Current Age				
	15	16	17	18	19
Black					
13[a]	.10%	.06%	.05%	.05%	.04%
14	.13	.11	.05	.04	.04
15	—	.19	.19	.08	.09
16	∸	—	.29	.24	.23
17	—	—	—	.30	.42
18	—	—	—	—	.47
White					
13[a]	.03%	.02%	.01%	.03%	.01%
14	.04	.02	.02	.02	.01
15	—	.06	.05	.04	.03
16	—	—	.13	.08	.08
17	—	—	—	.13	.13
18	—	—	—	—	.19

[a]Refers to the probability of having intercourse at ages 12 and 13.

whose current age is 15, has a 13 percent chance (P = .1287) of having had her first premarital intercourse at age 14, a 19-year-old black female has less than a 4 percent chance (P = .0366) of having had her first premarital intercourse when she was 14.

Almost without exception, reading across the rows of Table 2-5 shows the probabilities going down. The obvious suggestion is that premarital intercourse is beginning at younger ages. We cannot say whether the eventual level of premarital intercourse of those who are now 15 will exceed the level of those who are now 19, but, at least in the case of whites, this seems likely. A marked increase in the ultimate level of premarital intercourse among black women is less likely, since 80 percent of those now aged 19 already have had intercourse. However, since these data do suggest a tendency for sexual activities to start at an earlier age nowadays, it will be surprising if a rise in the overall prevalence of premarital intercourse does not result.

REFERENCE

ZELNIK, MELVIN, & KANTNER, JOHN F. 1973. "Sexuality, Contraception, and Pregnancy among Young Unwed Females in the United States." In *Demographic and Social Aspects of Population Growth*, Charles F. Westoff & Robert Parke, Jr., eds. Research Reports of the Commission on Population Growth and the American Future, Vol. 1. Washington: U.S. Government Printing Office.

3. Changes in Contraceptive Practices among Married Couples

When social historians of the future record the critical changes of the twentieth century in the United States, one of the most fundamental changes they will note is the modernization of fertility control. Although the abortion controversy has captured the headlines in recent years, a much more pervasive change has been taking place quietly in the contraceptive practices of American couples of all races, classes, and religions.

Data from the 1970 National Fertility Study reveal a dramatic drop in the rate of unwanted fertility between the 1961–1965 period and the 1966–1970 period—a decline of some 36 percent in the number of unwanted births per 1,000 woman-years of exposure to the risk of unwanted childbearing. The decline was 35 percent for whites, 56 percent for blacks. We estimate that about half of the nationwide fertility decline between the two periods is due to the improvement in the control of unwanted births (Ryder & Westoff, 1973). Such improvements can result from a number of factors—earlier or more extensive use of

"Changes in Contraceptive Practices among Married Couples" is based on data collected in the 1965 and 1970 National Fertility Studies co-directed by Charles F. Westoff and Norman B. Ryder. These studies were supported by the National Institute of Child Health and Human Development. The chapter is based in part on Westoff, Charles F., "The Modernization of U.S. Contraceptive Practice," *Family Planning Perspectives*, vol. 4, no. 3 (July 1972), pp. 9–12, and on Westoff, Charles F., and Larry L. Bumpass, "The Revolution in Birth Control Practices of U.S. Roman Catholics," *Science*, vol. 179, no. 4068 (January 5, 1973), pp. 41–44.

contraception; enlarged or more consistent use of the more effective medical methods; greater motivation to avoid pregnancy, possibly resulting in more regular contraceptive use or recourse to other means of fertility control; or some combination of such changes. This chapter will describe changes in the patterns of contraceptive use among married couples of reproductive age between 1965 and 1970, based on data drawn from the two National Fertility Studies in those years (Ryder & Westoff, 1971). These studies were based on extensive interviews conducted with national probability samples of 4,810 and 5,884 married and unmarried women, respectively, who were younger than 45. The analysis is confined to women currently married and living with their husbands.

CONTRACEPTIVE USE

Although the proportion who had never used contraception was small (16 percent), the proportion who were not currently using contraception in 1970 amounted to more than one-third of married couples of reproductive age, or nearly nine million couples (see Table 3-1). This included wives who were intentionally or accidentally pregnant, in the postpartum, or trying to become pregnant (amounting collectively to 14 percent in 1970); couples who were sterile or subfecund (13 percent); and those who were not using contraception for miscel-

TABLE 3-1. CURRENT EXPOSURE OF MARRIED[a] COUPLES TO THE RISK OF CONTRACEPTION: 1965 AND 1970

Type of Exposure	All Couples (Wife under 45)		Younger Couples (Wife under 30)		Older Couples (Wife 30 to 44)	
	1965	1970	1965	1970	1965	1970
(Number of couples)	(4,810)	(5,884)	(1,918)	(2,743)	(2,892)	(3,141)
Percent total	100%	100%	100%	100%	100%	100%
Using contraceptives	64	65	64	66	64	64
Not using contraceptives	36	35	37	34	36	36
Pregnant, postpartum, or trying to get pregnant	14	14	25	24	7	6
Sterile and subfecund[b]	14	13	5	4	21	20
Other nonusers	8	8	6	6	8	9

[a]Currently living together.

[b]Includes those reporting sterilizing operations (for noncontraceptive reasons) and those who reported that it was not physically possible to have another child.

laneous other reasons (8 percent). The proportion not using contraception declined very slightly from 36 percent in 1965 to 35 percent in 1970, a drop concentrated entirely among younger couples and reflecting mainly a decrease in the proportions pregnant, postpartum, or trying to become pregnant.

Although there was little change in the overall proportion of couples using contraception—64 percent in 1965 and 65 percent in 1970, there were significant changes in the methods used (Table 3-2). An increase in the proportion of couples sterilized for contraceptive reasons is apparent among older couples. All couples showed an increase in use of the pill, the IUD, and foam and a decrease in the use of all other methods. Excluded from this tabulation are many couples who had used or who will use contraception, but who were not using any contraceptive method in 1965 or 1970.

Contraceptive Sterilization

One of the most dramatic findings in the 1970 National Fertility Study is the fact that voluntary sterilization—typically, tubal ligation for women and vasectomy for men—has become the most popular method of contraception among older couples (those in which the wife is aged 30–44). One-quarter of all older couples practicing contraception had been surgically sterilized; the operations were almost equally divided between men and women. The corresponding figure in 1965 was 16 percent. Included are all surgical procedures reported by the women to have been elected for contraceptive reasons; other forms of surgery that produce sterility but that were performed for other reasons are excluded. The closest competitor is the pill, which is used by 21 percent of older couples (an increase of eight percentage points over 1965). The jump in reliance on surgical procedures, and the fact that contraceptive sterilization had by 1970 become the most popular method among older couples, appears to reflect the unsuitability of other methods of contraception for many couples who have already had all the children they want. It is estimated that as of 1970 some 2.75 million couples of reproductive age had resorted to sterilization, which is usually regarded as an extreme solution to the problem of fertility control.

Reliance on contraceptive sterilization is evidently more common among black women than among white women, but much less so among black men than among white men. Although almost one-third (32 percent) of older black women (compared with 12 percent of older white women) report having been sterilized, only 2 percent of older black men (compared with 13 percent of older white men) were re-

TABLE 3-2. METHODS OF CONTRACEPTION CURRENTLY USED BY MARRIED[a] COUPLES: 1965 AND 1970

	All Couples (Wife under 45)						Younger Couples (Wife under 30)						Older Couples (Wife 30 to 44)					
	Total[b]		White		Black		Total		White		Black		Total		White		Black	
Current method	1965	1970	1965	1970	1965	1970	1965	1970	1965	1970	1965	1970	1965	1970	1965	1970	1965	1970
(Number of users)	(3,032)	(3,810)	(2,441)	(3,273)	(554)	(462)	(1,215)	(1,800)	(922)	(1,540)	(276)	(222)	(1,817)	(2,010)	(1,513)	(1,733)	(278)	(240)
Percent total	100%	100%	100%	100%	100%	100%	100%	100%	100%	100%	100%	100%	100%	100%	100%	100%	100%	100%
Wife sterilized[c]	7	8	6	8	14	19	3	3	3	3	7	5	9	13	8	12	22	32
Husband sterilized[d]	5	8	5	8	1	1	3	3	3	3	—[d]	—[d]	6	12	7	13	1	2
Pill[e]	24	34	24	34	22	37	41	49	42	49	31	54	13	21	13	20	13	22
IUD[f]	1	7	1	7	3	8	2	9	1	9	5	10	1	6	1	6	1	5
Diaphragm[g]	10	6	10	6	5	5	6	4	7	4	3	4	12	8	13	8	7	7
Condom[h]	22	14	22	15	17	7	19	11	19	12	18	6	24	17	24	17	16	7
Withdrawal	4	4	3	4	2	1	2	2	2	2	2	—[d]	5	2	5	3	4	1
Foam	3	6	3	6	6	6	5	8	4	8	8	7	2	4	2	4	4	5
Rhythm[i]	11	6	12	7	2	2	7	4	8	4	3	1	13	8	14	9	2	2
Douche	5	3	4	3	17	8	5	2	4	2	15	6	5	4	4	4	20	10
Other[f]	7	5	7	4	10	6	6	4	6	4	8	7	8	5	8	5	12	6

[a] Currently living together.

[b] Includes nonwhites other than blacks.

[c] Surgical procedures undertaken at least partly for contraceptive reasons.

[d] Less than 1 percent.

[e] Includes combination with any other method.

[f] Includes combination with any other method except pill.

[g] Includes combination with any method except pill or IUD.

[h] Includes combination with any method except pill, IUD, or diaphragm.

[i] Includes other multiple as well as simple methods and a small percentage of unreported methods.

ported to have had vasectomies. These figures point up differences between whites and blacks in two different areas. On the one hand, they suggest that the black woman bears a greater share of the responsibility for fertility control, which is further supported by the fact that the so-called "male" methods—the condom and withdrawal —are used much less frequently by blacks than by whites. On the other hand, there is also considerable difference between black and white women in their belief that a vasectomy will impair male sexual ability: 36 percent of black women, compared with 13 percent of white women, held such beliefs in 1970 (Presser & Bumpass, 1972). This difference appears to be primarily the result of educational differences.

Adding the two types of operations together shows that sterilization is more common among older black couples (34 percent) than among older white couples (25 percent). Probably the best interpretation of this fact is that the more effective medical methods of contraception are less available to younger blacks, which in turn leads to greater desperation by older black women to control fertility. However, as the dramatic increase in the proportion of younger blacks using the pill and the IUD reveals, this situation is changing rapidly.

The Pill

In 1970, nearly six million married women of reproductive age were using the oral contraceptive—more than one out of every five. The pill is by far the most popular method of contraception. It accounted for 34 percent of all contraceptive practice in 1970, taking a commanding lead over all other methods (see Table 3-2). Its closest competitor was contraceptive sterilization (16 percent).

The adoption of the pill by American women has been an amazing phenomenon, considering the various side effects associated with its use, and is an indication of the large market for effective contraception. The pill made its first public appearance in 1960. By 1965, 24 percent of married women who were practicing contraception were using the pill; by 1970 this proportion had grown to 34 percent. Most of this increase can be attributed to its widespread acceptance by young women. In 1970 about half of all younger women (49 percent) using contraception were relying on the pill, compared with 21 percent of older women. The growth in popularity of the method has been especially pronounced among young black women; between 1965 and 1970 its use increased from 31 to 54 percent (see Table 3-2).

The IUD

About 1.25 million married women in the United States—one out of every 20 couples of reproductive age—now use the highly effective intrauterine device. Although the IUD's popularity is still far below that of the pill, its use grew from 1 percent of all wives who were practicing contraception in 1965 to 7 percent by 1970 (Table 3-2). In 1970 black and white women relied on the method about equally. Although IUD use increased among both younger and older women, it has proven somewhat more popular among wives younger than 30 (9 percent) than among those 30–44 (6 percent).

Other Methods

The sharp increases in reliance on contraceptive sterilization and on the use of the pill and the IUD naturally caused the use of the older methods to decline accordingly. The use of all the older methods declined over the five-year period: the condom declined in use from 22 percent in 1965 to 14 percent by 1970, the diaphragm from 10 to 6 percent, rhythm from 11 to 6 percent. Other methods, including withdrawal and douche, also declined (see Table 3-2). Thus, whereas 59 percent were using conventional methods (other than foam, which is a newer method) in 1965, only 36 percent were in 1970.

THE REVOLUTION AMONG U.S. CATHOLICS

The 1968 Papal Encyclical ended the period of ambiguity and speculation about the Roman Catholic Church's position on birth control by reaffirming the traditional ban on methods of contraception other than the rhythm method. Since that time there has been considerable interest in how American Catholics would respond. The trend toward nonconformity that was documented in the 1965 National Fertility Study (Ryder & Westoff, 1971), the observed reduction in the rate of unwanted fertility over the decade among all groups, including Catholics (Ryder & Westoff, 1973), and the sharp decline in U.S. fertility rates—all combine to enhance the plausibility of the hypothesis that Catholic couples have increasingly adopted unapproved methods of contraception. An earlier analysis, based on follow-up interviews with Catholic women from the 1965 Study, supported this view (Westoff & Ryder, 1970).

The present analysis is based on currently married white Catholic women who are living with their husbands. Data for this subsample of the 1970 National Fertility Study are analyzed in conjunction with comparable women in the 1965 National Fertility Study and from two earlier U.S. fertility surveys conducted in 1955 (Freedman, Whelpton & Campbell, 1959) and 1960 (Whelpton, Campbell & Patterson, 1966).

Concepts and Measures

Although "current use" is the appropriate measure for describing the contraceptive protection of the population at a given point in time, "most recent use" is more appropriate for measuring *usual* contraceptive practices. At any given time, many couples are not using any method simply because they are pregnant, trying to become pregnant, or in postpartum. Others may not be using for a variety of temporary reasons such as illness, involuntary sterility, or temporary separation. It is the *usual* method of contraception that is most relevant to the issue of Catholic conformity. Of course, some couples not currently using a method will change methods when they begin using again. To the extent that such changes are away from conformity (as seems most likely), our measure understates the level of nonconformity.

The concept of "conformity" is defined here in terms of the traditional norm of the Catholic Church (reaffirmed by the encyclical) prohibiting the use of any method of fertility control other than periodic continence, the so-called rhythm method. There are two categories of Catholic women who are classified as conforming to Church doctrine: those who have never used any method of contraception and those whose most recent practice was the rhythm method.

The Trend in Catholic Conformity

By linking the 1955 and 1960 Growth of American Family Studies with the 1965 and 1970 National Fertility Studies, we can observe the trend in Catholic conformity over a 15-year period. There has been a dramatic change in the adherence of Catholic women to the Church's teaching on birth control. The proportion of Catholic women 18–39 years of age using methods of contraception other than rhythm has increased from 30 percent in 1955 to 68 percent by 1970, with the greatest changes occurring in the last five years. Between 1965 and 1970 the percentage of Catholic women deviating from official teaching on birth control rose from one-half to two-thirds. It seems clear that the Papal

Encyclical has not retarded the increasing defection of Catholic women in this area of teaching.

This trend is even more apparent when examined by age and year of birth across all four studies (see the vertical comparisons in Table 3-3). There has been a spectacular increase in nonconformity

TABLE 3-3. PROPORTION OF MARRIED WHITE CATHOLIC WOMEN NOT CONFORMING TO CHURCH TEACHING ON BIRTH CONTROL: 1955, 1960, 1965, AND 1970 (BY AGE AND BIRTH COHORT)[a]

| Birth Cohort | Age | | | | |
	20-24	25-29	30-34	35-39	40-44
1916-20				28	45
1921-25			30	46	43
1926-30		37	40	52	50
1931-35	30	40	50	50	
1936-40	43	54	68		
1941-45	51	74			
1946-50	78				

[a]In the 1955 and 1960 studies (on the top and second diagonals, respectively) a woman is classified as not conforming to Church teaching if she had ever used any method of contraception other than rhythm. In the 1965 and 1970 data (third and bottom diagonals, respectively) the classification relates to the method most recently used.

among Catholic women at the youngest ages. Among women 20–24 in the year of each study, the proportion not conforming was 30 percent in 1955, 43 percent five years later, 51 percent by 1965, and 78 percent by 1970. The increase from 1955 to 1970 was almost as steep for the next two age groups: from 37 to 74 percent and from 30 to 68 percent for ages 25–29 and 30–34, respectively.

The increase in nonconformity that occurs as women grow older is revealed by the horizontal comparisons in Table 3-3. For example, of Catholic women born between 1936 and 1940, 43 percent were deviating from Church teaching by age 20–24 in 1960, 54 percent by age 25–29 in 1965, and 68 percent were not conforming by the time this cohort had reached 30–34 years of age in 1970. It is not surprising that women tend to adopt more effective methods as they grow older. As a cohort ages, increasing proportions have had all of the children they want and thus face the risk of unwanted pregnancies. In this light, it is interesting to speculate about the ultimate nonconformity of the youngest women in these studies. Women who were 20–24 in 1970 were already at the 78 percent level and it seems likely that their deviation from the Church will become indistinguishable from that of non-Catholics, reaching a near maximum of around 90 percent. (The remaining 10 percent is comprised of those who discover subfecundity before ever using contraception, and thus never use any method, and a small fraction who use rhythm successfully.)

Religiousness

It is important to determine whether the increase in nonconformity between 1965 and 1970 is the result of attrition from the Church in general or of rejection of the prohibition against birth control in particular. Our analysis seems to indicate that both trends are occurring: that Catholic women (and presumably men as well) *are* moving away from traditional formal practice, and that those women who do continue formal practice are increasingly ignoring Church teaching on birth control.

It should be emphasized at the outset that we have not undertaken any extensive or intensive study of Catholic religious practices or attitudes. Our conclusions are based on only one index of religious behavior, though a very significant measure: the frequency of receiving Holy Communion. We have divided the women into two categories: those who receive Communion at least once a month and those who receive it less frequently. Since receiving Communion at least once a month exceeds the minimal requirement to remain in good standing within the Church, this dichotomy differentiates between Catholics who adhere closely to their faith and those whose attachment is weak or even nominal.

The proportion of Catholic women who receive Communion at least monthly has decreased from 52 percent in 1965 to 44 percent in 1970. Most of this change has been concentrated among the younger women, among whom the proportion receiving Communion monthly or more frequently declined from 52 to 37 percent.

Overall, nonconformity increased by 16 percent between 1965 and 1970 (from 49 to 65 percent). If there had been no change in the proportion of women receiving Communion regularly, the increase in nonconformity would have been 14 percent. Thus, the change due to declining religiousness is fairly small, amounting to about one-eighth of the overall increase in nonconformity. This is also true among younger women, whose deviation from Church teaching on birth control has been greatest; only 2 percent of the 24 percent increase in nonconformity can be attributed to a decline in religious practice.

Consequently, the primary factor accounting for the increase in nonconformity is a willingness to deviate from Church teaching on this particular issue. The majority (53 percent) of the more religious Catholics in 1970 were deviating from the official position on birth control, a remarkable increase from the 33 percent in 1965 (see Table 3-4). Even more remarkable, and perhaps an indication of further

TABLE 3-4. PROPORTION OF MARRIED WHITE CATHOLIC WOMEN WHO HAVE NEVER USED ANY METHOD OR WHOSE MOST RECENT METHOD USED WAS RHYTHM, THE PILL, OR OTHER METHODS: 1965 AND 1970 (BY AGE AND FREQUENCY OF RECEIVING COMMUNION)

Most Recent Practice	All Couples (Wife under 45)		Younger Couples (Wife under 30)		Older Couples (Wife 30 to 44)	
	1965	1970	1965	1970	1965	1970
Percent receiving communion monthly or more	100% ·	100%	100%	100%	100%	100%
Never used	25	23	24	15	25	29
Rhythm	42	23	38	18	45	27
Pill	11	26	20	37	5	18
Other methods	22	27	18	30	25	26
Percent not conforming	33%	53%	38%	67%	30%	44%
(Number of couples)	(558)	(544)	(207)	(221)	(351)	(323)
Percent receiving communion less than monthly	100%	100%	100%	100%	100%	100%
Never used	21	17	22	14	20	21
Rhythm	12	8	12	5	12	11
Pill	14	30	28	39	6	19
Other methods	53	45	39	41	61	48
Percent not conforming	67%	75%	66%	81%	67%	68%
(Number of couples)	(525)	(706)	(194)	(378)	(331)	(328)

changes to come, is the increase in nonconformity among the younger, more religious Catholic women: from 38 percent in 1965 to 67 percent by 1970. The corresponding increase among older religious Catholics was from 30 to 44 percent, a substantial change in itself.

Among less religious Catholics there has been an increase in non-conformity only in the younger generation—from 66 percent in 1965 to 81 percent in 1970. Only the older, less religious Catholics showed no change in conformity over the five-year period: at both times some two-thirds were not conforming to Church teaching on birth control.

The pill has played a major role in the decreasing conformity of the more religious Catholic women. Among women under 30, its use increased from 20 percent in 1965 to 37 percent in 1970. Almost exactly the reverse occurred for the rhythm method, which declined in use from 38 percent in 1965 to 18 percent in 1970. There was also a significant decrease in the proportion of religious women in the younger generation who had never used any method (from 24 percent in 1965 to 15 percent in 1970) and an increase in those using unapproved methods other than the pill (from 18 to 30 percent). Most of this latter increase is due to the adoption of the newer methods—the IUD and foam.

Among older women the more religious Catholics shifted away from rhythm toward the pill, but among the less religious women of this generation the increase in the popularity of the pill was at the expense of methods other than rhythm.

The Convergence of Religious Differences

One consequence of the increasing nonconformity of Catholics has been to diminish the differences between Catholic and non-Catholic contraceptive practices. In the five-year period between 1965 and 1970 a marked convergence has occurred in the proportions using every method except surgical sterilization. The blurring of the Catholic/non-Catholic difference is most evident among younger couples, which suggests that the differential for all couples will diminish even further in the years ahead. It does not seem at all unlikely that by the end of the decade Catholics and non-Catholics will be very similar in their birth-control practices. Indeed, if 10 percent more of the young Catholic women who have never used any method or who are currently using rhythm shift to the pill, and this is certainly the trend of the times, the contraceptive practices of Catholics and non-Catholics in this country will become virtually indistinguishable. The only exception would be the presumably continuing greater reliance of non-Catholics on surgical sterilization.

SUMMARY AND CONCLUSIONS

The net result of all of these changes in methods has been a significant increase in the use of more effective contraception, which is undoubtedly the main explanation for the decline in the rate of unwanted fertility between 1965 and 1970 and a major factor in the drop in the nation's birthrate. The three most effective methods—sterilization, the pill, and the IUD—have increased from 37.2 percent of all contraceptive practice in 1965 to 57.9 percent in 1970. If we add to these three methods the very effective diaphragm, condom, and a small fraction of multiple-method usage, about four out of five couples using contraception in 1970 were highly protected from the risk of unintentional conception. This high level of protection is now being experienced by both blacks and whites.

Over the past two decades there has been a widespread and increasing defection by Roman Catholic women from the traditional teaching of the Church on the subject of birth control and a resulting convergence of Catholic and non-Catholic contraceptive practices. By 1970 two-thirds of all Catholic women were using methods disapproved by the Church; this figure reached three-quarters for women under 30 years of age. Considering the fact that most of the one-quarter of young Catholic women conforming to Church teaching had not yet used any method, the ultimate proportion deviating may well reach 90 percent as these women grow older and the problems of fertility control become more important.

Perhaps the most significant finding is that the defection has been most pronounced among the more religious Catholics, women who receive Communion at least once a month. Even among this group, the majority now deviates from Church teaching on birth control; among the younger, more religious Catholics the proportion not conforming reaches two-thirds.

It seems abundantly clear that U.S. Catholics have rejected the 1968 Papal Encyclical and that a wide gulf exists between the behavior of most Catholic women and the position of the more conservative clergy and the official stand of the Church itself.

Ultimately this crisis of authority will probably be resolved by a change in official teaching, since it seems doubtful that such a major discrepancy can continue indefinitely without other repercussions. At a minimum, the cost to the Roman Catholic Church will be a loss of authority in a major area of life—that of sex and reproduction.

REFERENCES

FREEDMAN, R.; WHELPTON, P. K.; & CAMPBELL, A. A. 1959. *Family Planning, Sterility and Population Growth.* New York: McGraw-Hill.

PRESSER, H. B., & BUMPASS, L. L. 1973. "Demographic and Social Aspects of Contraceptive Sterilization in the United States: 1965–1970." In *Demographic and Social Aspects of Population Growth,* Charles F. Westoff & Robert Parke, Jr., eds. Research Reports of the Commission on Population Growth and the American Future, Vol. 1. Washington: U.S. Government Printing Office, pp. 505–68.

RYDER, N. B., & WESTOFF, C. F. 1971. *Reproduction in the United States: 1965*. Princeton, N.J.: Princeton University Press.

————. 1973. "Wanted and Unwanted Fertility in the United States: 1965 and 1970." In *Demographic and Social Aspects of Population Growth*, Charles F. Westoff & Robert Parke, Jr., eds. Research Reports of the Commission on Population Growth and the American Future, Vol. 1. Washington: U.S. Government Printing Office, pp. 467–87.

WESTOFF, C. F., & RYDER, N. B. 1970. "United States: The Papal Encyclical and Catholic Practice and Attitudes, 1969." In *Studies in Family Planning*, no. 50 (February 1970), pp. 1–7.

WHELPTON, P. K.; CAMPBELL, A. A.; and PATTERSON, J. E. 1966. *Fertility and Family Planning in the United States*. Princeton, N.J.: Princeton University Press.

LARRY L. BUMPASS | HARRIET B. PRESSER ══════════

4. *The Increasing Acceptance*
of Sterilization and Abortion

In the last decade, the United States has experienced a revolution in
the nature of fertility control. Using traditional "effective" methods
of contraception, many couples were able to delay or reduce the number of accidental or unwanted pregnancies, but not prevent these altogether. It has been estimated that nearly half of the couples using the
condom or diaphragm to prevent unwanted pregnancy fail within a
five-year period (Ryder & Westoff, 1971). A major reason for this high
level of failure is that these methods require attention at each act of
coitus, and thus are often omitted. The unprecedented diffusion of
the oral contraceptive not only improved protection against accidental
pregnancy, but also separated contraception from coitus. As a result,
significant proportions of the population have come to expect complete

Larry L. Bumpass is an associate professor of sociology and a member of the
staff of the Center for Demography and Ecology at the University of Wisconsin.
Formerly he was on the research staff of the Office of Population Research at Princeton University. He has specialized in research on American fertility and marriage.

Harriet B. Presser is an associate professor of sociomedical science in the
School of Public Health at Columbia University. She formerly worked for the
Population Council, where she specialized in the study of the social and demo-
graphic aspects of sterilization.

"The Increasing Acceptance of Sterilization and Abortion" copyright © 1973
by Larry L. Bumpass and Harriet B. Presser. This essay is based on research done
for the President's Commission on Population Growth and the American Future
and published in Research Reports of the Commission. Portions of the research
have also been published in "Contraceptive Sterilization in the U.S.: 1965 and 1970,"
in *Demography*, Vol. 9, no. 4 (November 1972), pp. 531–48.

and unobtrusive fertility control. However, many have grown concerned about the consequence of long-term administration of the pill; others are unable to use the pill for medical reasons.

In this context, it should not be surprising that two formerly disapproved methods of contraception—sterilization and abortion—have been rapidly gaining acceptance among the U.S. population. In this chapter, we survey the increasing acceptance of these methods, both in attitude and in practice, and consider briefly the demographic implications of these trends.

CONTRACEPTIVE STERILIZATION

Until recently contraceptive sterilization was generally disapproved of and relatively infrequent in the U.S. Its acceptance may have been limited by widespread misinformation about the physiological consequences as well as by the ways it differs from other contraceptive methods.

Misunderstanding of the physiological consequences of sterilization appears to be extensive in the United States. One recent study of a college population showed substantial proportions of both students and faculty (including the biology faculty) understood neither the nature of the operation nor its effects (Eisner et al., 1970). It is not surprising, then, that the belief that vasectomy impairs male sexual ability was still prevalent in several segments of the population in 1970 (Presser & Bumpass, 1972). There may be misapprehensions about the physiological effects of female sterilization as well.

Sterilization is unlike other forms of contraception in that it is a means of *ending* reproduction, not of *delaying* it. Persons who choose to be sterilized must be confident of their decision to have no more children in the future. Several factors may lend uncertainty to this decision. Among them are the possibility of marital dissolution and remarriage, and the chance of infant or child mortality. Another reason why sterilization may be avoided is that it involves a surgical procedure. In addition to the usual anxiety attached to any operation, sterilization is usually not covered by health insurance programs.

The finality of sterilization has led many physicians to be extremely cautious about performing the operation for contraceptive reasons. Until 1969, the medical profession had established standards for the practice of female sterilization that specified minimum age levels and number of children for contraceptive operations. The 1965 official manual of the American College of Obstetricians and Gynecologists suggested that contraceptive sterilization be performed on women under 25 years of age only if they had five living children. Women 30 years old needed four children, and women over 35 needed three living children to qualify. The 1969 official manual dropped all references to age and number of children and many hospitals have changed their practices accordingly. The relaxing of restrictions by the medical profession and the increasing approval and prevalence of sterilization have undoubtedly had a mutually reinforcing influence on one another. For persons considering sterilization, the knowledge that the operation is readily available and that their friends and relatives do not disapprove may make sterilization more likely. At the same time, the satisfaction of increasing numbers of sterilized persons could do much to dispel fears and combat misinformation about the operation and to further increase its approval.

We report here on changes in attitudes toward, and in the practice of, contraceptive sterilization in the United States as measured in the 1965 and 1970 National Fertility Studies. The 1965 data collection procedures are described in detail in the published account of that study (Ryder & Westoff, 1971). For our present purposes the data are restricted to married women under age 45, whose husbands are present. (4,810 women in 1965 and 5,884 women in 1970.)*

Increasing Approval of Sterilization

There is no question that attitudes toward sterilization have become more favorable (see Table 4-1). The proportion approving of male sterilization increased from 34 percent in 1965 to 52 percent in 1970. Since the proportion "neutral" on the subject also increased, the decline of disapproval was even more substantial: from 61 percent to 31 percent of the population. Similar changes also occurred in attitudes toward female sterilization: the proportion approving was 37 percent in 1965 and 54 percent in 1970; disapproval declined from slightly over one-half to just over one-quarter of the population.

There are important differences by race, however, both in the amount of change occurring and in the relative evaluation of female and male sterilization. During the five-year period, approval increased more rapidly among white women than among black women, particularly approval of male sterilization. In 1965 white women were only slightly more likely to approve of male sterilization than were black women. By 1970 male sterilization was approved by 54 percent of white females, but only 34 percent of black females. Similar, though

* These data are analyzed in more detail in our report to the Commission on Population Growth and the American Future (Presser & Bumpass, 1972).

TABLE 4-1. PERCENT APPROVING MALE AND FEMALE
STERILIZATION: 1965 AND 1970 (BY RACE, EDUCATION,
AND RELIGION AMONG WHITES)

	Approving Male Sterilization		Approving Female Sterilization		(Number of Cases)	
	1965	1970	1965	1970	1965	1970
Total	34%	52%	37%	54%	(4,756)	(5,875)
Race						
White	34	54	37	55	(3,735)	(4,968)
Black	30	34	39	46	(951)	(780)
Education						
Under 12 years	32	43	37	48	(1,813)	(1,617)
12 years	34	52	36	54	(2,090)	(2,749)
College	36	62	43	61	(851)	(1,509)
Religion among whites						
Non-Catholic	42	59	44	60	(2,525)	(3,609)
Mixed Catholic	24	47	32	49	(326)	(321)
Both Catholic	17	40	20	39	(882)	(1,015)

smaller, differences appear for female sterilization. By 1970, 55 percent
of white women, compared with 46 percent of black women, approved
of female sterilization.

There are also important educational and religious differences in
the approval of sterilization, with the highest approval among college-
educated women and among non-Catholics. In 1970 over 60 percent of
college-educated women approved of both male and female sterilization; only one-sixth disapproved.

Approval of sterilization is also influenced by women's fertility
histories. For example, approval was found to be relatively high among
women who did not want more children and who thus faced the risk
of unwanted pregnancy. Approval was even higher among women who
had already experienced an unwanted birth.

In addition to general attitude questions, respondents in 1970
were asked whether they would seriously consider such an operation
for themselves. Their responses to these questions indicate substantial
interest in the operation, especially among the currently nonsterile
who have had as many children as they want. Forty-four percent of
those who did not want more children said they would seriously consider an operation for themselves; over a third said they thought their
husbands would seriously consider vasectomy.

Increasing Prevalence of Sterilization

Not only have attitudes been changing, but the practice of sterilization has substantially increased as well. Between 1965 and 1970, there was a 38 percent increase in the proportion of the population who had undergone contraceptive sterilization. By 1970, one of every ten American couples with the husband present and the wife under 45 years of age had chosen sterilization as a contraceptive method. Slightly over 2.75 million couples had been sterilized by 1970—almost one-half of these by vasectomy.

However, sterilization is a viable option only for women who do not intend to have more children. Thus, since there were proportionately more young women in 1970 than in 1965, the above figures conceal some of the real increase in the choice of this method. Measured as a proportion of the population at risk (thereby excluding those who intend to have more children or are sterile for other reasons), the prevalence of contraceptive sterilization increased impressively from 12 to 18 percent between 1965 and 1970 (see Table 4-2). Thus, among couples in 1970 for whom sterilization had been a viable option, one out of every six had chosen this method of contraception. In addition, there is clear indication that the increase in sterilization is accelerating: most of the 1965–70 increase occurred during the last two years of that period. There are important differences by race in the type of sterilization, although the total proportion sterilized is only slightly higher among blacks than among whites. Vasectomies are the predominant mode of sterilization among whites, but they are extremely rare among blacks.

There is also considerable regional variation in the practice of sterilization. In both 1965 and 1970, contraceptive sterilization was most prevalent in the West. However, increases during this five-year period were greater in the other regions and were especially large for blacks in the Northeast, among whom contraceptive sterilization rose from 6 to 19 percent of the population at risk. In 1970 the prevalence of sterilization was lowest in the Northeast (11 percent of those at risk) and highest in the West (27 percent of those at risk).

One important component of the increase in sterilization has been couples who have already experienced unwanted fertility and feel that sterilization is their "last resort." For example, although sterilization increased among women of all parities between 1965 and 1970, the increase was most marked among women with six or more children: from 21 to 31 percent of the population at risk among whites, and from 27 to 47 percent of the population at risk among blacks.

TABLE 4-2. PERCENT OF RISK POPULATION[a] WITH
CONTRACEPTIVE STERILIZATION: 1965 AND 1970
(BY RACE, EDUCATION, AND RELIGION AMONG
WHITES)

	All Operations[b]		Vasectomies		Tubal Ligations		(Number of Cases)	
	1965	1970	1965	1970	1965	1970	1965	1970
Total	12%	18%	5%	8%	6%	7%	(2,963)	(3,427)
Race								
White	12	18	6	9	5	6	(2,304)	(2,901)
Black	14	21	—	1	12	15	(617)	(460)
Education								
Under 12 years	14	24	5	7	8	13	(1,242)	(980)
12 years	12	16	6	8	5	5	(1,236)	(1,633)
College	12	18	6	10	4	6	(485)	(814)
Religion among whites								
Non-Catholic	15	21	7	11	6	7	(1,622)	(2,194)
Mixed Catholic	10	8	3	4	5	3	(204)	(162)
Both Catholic	6	8	2	3	3	4	(478)	(545)

[a]Couples intending to have no more children and not involuntarily sterile.

[b]In addition to vasectomies and tubal ligations, includes hysterectomies and other operations, as well as couples reporting more than one operation.

The prevalence of sterilization also differs according to education and religion. Previous studies have indicated either that the proportion sterilized is highest among those with the least education or that there is a curvilinear relationship between education and the proportion sterilized (Phillips, 1971; Presser, in press). Table 4-2 shows that the direction of the educational differences in sterilization differs by type of sterilization. Whereas the relationship with education is inverse for tubal ligations, it is direct for vasectomies. These differences may result from educational differences in the willingness of a husband to become sterilized, from misinformation about the physiological effects of vasectomy, or from differences in medical access to the two types of sterilization. As a consequence of these differences, vasectomies were the predominant form of contraceptive sterilization in 1970 for all but the lowest education group.

In light of the Catholic Church's stance on contraception in general, it is not surprising to find that in 1970 the prevalence of contraceptive sterilization was twice as high among couples who were both Protestant than among those who were both Catholic. Mixed Protestant-Catholic couples were indistinguishable with respect to sterilization from couples in which both spouses were Catholic. Even though there was a moderate increase in sterilization among Catholics, the rapid acceptance of sterilization by Protestant couples caused the religious differences in the prevalence of sterilization to increase between 1965 and 1970.

An analysis of recent contraceptive sterilizations reveals that sterilization is not largely confined to people in their late childbearing years. Nearly 10 percent of recent sterilizations, both male and female, occurred before the wife was 25 years of age, and almost another 30 percent occurred when the wife was between 25 and 29 years old. Twenty percent of the husbands were under 30 years of age when either they or their wives were sterilized; 50 percent were under 35. This relatively early timing of sterilization is not simply the result of women having many children at an early age; over 50 percent had no more than three children.

Demographic Implications of Increasing Sterilization

We have documented a rather impressive increase between 1965 and 1970 in the use of contraceptive sterilization, a trend that was common to virtually all subgroups considered. However, the extent to which this trend affects fertility depends upon the nature of the alternatives available and the extent to which sterilized couples would have opted for these alternatives had they not been sterilized. Since contraceptive sterilization is a means of ending reproduction, its major demographic impact must be evaluated in terms of the reduction of unwanted fertility. If unwanted fertility were to become quite low without sterilization, then the proportion sterilized would make little difference in demographic terms. Our best guess is that this might soon be the case. Preliminary analysis of the 1970 National Fertility Study indicates a continued trend toward use of the pill and the intrauterine device (IUD), especially among the young. In addition, it appears that induced abortion (to be considered in the following section) will play an ever-increasing role as a back-up measure to prevent unwanted births when contraception fails. Indeed, the increasing acceptance of sterilization is viewed here as part of the more general revolution in fertility control. Couples who turn away from other effective methods after achieving their desired family size undoubtedly want an equally effective method, but one with minimal side-effects. Sterilization meets this need.

To point out that in *demographic* terms increasing sterilization may have only a slight *net* impact over and above other modern methods is not to suggest that the trend toward sterilization is of little importance. It is important precisely because sterilization is one of the most effective contraceptive methods, and for many couples the most preferable. In our 1970 sample, over half of those recently sterilized had used the pill or the IUD as their most recent contraceptive method. Of those who had used another method since their last birth, two-thirds were pill or IUD users. Since the majority of these couples chose sterilization after having had recent experience with one of the other modern methods, they probably would have been more likely than the population at large to use modern methods if sterilization had not been possible. (However, some may have been so strongly dissatisfied with these other methods that they would have turned to less effective methods in the absence of sterilization.)

In short, a growing incidence of sterilization does not have as marked a demographic impact in a society with modern fertility control as it might in one with a less effective contraceptive regime, such as Puerto Rico (Presser, in press). This is not to make light of its importance as the most effective of the modern methods available. Its particular advantages are that it involves neither continued motivation nor continued side-effects. Moreover, unlike the pill and the IUD, sterilization has the advantage that both its short- and long-term physiological effects are known. The major drawback of sterilization is that reversibility cannot be assured. If sterilization methods with near-certain reversibility could be developed, allowing the use of sterilization for long-term childspacing and eliminating anxiety over the finality of the decision to have no more children, this method would likely become the dominant means of fertility control. Even in the current situation it has become the most popular method currently used by couples in which the wife is aged 30–44 (Westoff, 1972).

INDUCED ABORTION

Whereas voluntary sterilization is a means of ending reproduction, abortion may be used for childspacing as well. Abortion is therefore an option over more of the life cycle than is sterilization. Although we are considering these methods separately, it should be noted that the prevalence of one may affect the prevalence of the other. For some couples, ready access to abortion may reduce interest in sterilization; for others, having had an abortion may make sterilization seem more desirable. At the same time, sterilization may avert subsequent abortions by preventing unwanted pregnancies. It is significant that the practice of both methods has been increasing in recent years.

The sources of recent changes in attitudes and practices with respect to abortion are numerous and complexly interrelated. At least four factors seem important here. First, as noted at the beginning of this chapter, the diffusion of the pill has increased the expectation of effective fertility control. One consequence of this marked improvement in ability to avoid accidental pregnancies may well be an erosion of social rationalizations about parenthood. Popular myths that halo even accidental pregnancies may weaken when such an event is no longer regarded as an inevitable fact of life. Thus, women may be more inclined than ever before to opt for abortion when an accidental pregnancy occurs.

A second factor is the growing concern with equality of opportunity for women, a phenomenon that is likely both a consequence and a cause of the above trend. The pill has given women the realistic option of making a commitment to nonfamilial roles. It has thus set the stage for a growing receptivity to demands for equality of opportunity. At the same time, the women's movement has placed great emphasis on achieving unhindered access to abortion so that accidental pregnancy will no longer interfere with women's careers.

Third, the changing legal status of abortion, both in response to the demands of women for complete fertility control and in the attempt to ameliorate the health consequences of high levels of illegal abortion, has played an undeniable role in changing abortion attitudes and practice.

Finally, the increasing employment of suction procedures for abortion has decreased the risk involved and made abortion on an ambulatory basis both safe and feasible.

Increasing Approval of Abortion

Decline in the opposition to abortion has been documented on the basis of five Gallup polls (Blake, 1970). Some of the questions asked in the 1965 and 1970 National Fertility Studies enable us to make a more detailed analysis of this trend. These data demonstrate that whether or not a person approves of abortion depends heavily upon the supposed reasons involved. Jones and Westoff (1972) report important increases in permissiveness toward abortion for so-called "soft" reasons. Approval in the case of danger to the mother's health apparently approached its upper limit in 1965 (over 90 percent), but absolute increases in approval for the other reasons ranged between 14 and 20 percent. There were two- to threefold increases in approval of abortion because of not wanting a child, if the woman were not married, or if the couple could not afford another child.

In 1970, approval of abortion for each reason was higher among non-Catholics than among Catholics. However, Catholics were not by any means unequivocally opposed to abortion. For example, 82 percent approved in the case of danger to the mother's health and 63 percent approved in the case of rape. Overall, blacks are slightly less favorable to abortion than whites. Approval of abortion increases markedly with the level of the wife's education.

When the question was put in personal terms, about 16 percent of the respondents said that they would seriously consider abortion for themselves in the case of unwanted pregnancy. This is about the same proportion as responses supporting abortion for any reason. However, the authors feel that the proportion supporting abortion for any reason is a considerable underestimate of the support for abortion on demand, because the question is directed at the behavior of other persons rather than at the medical-legal context of that behavior; that is, many people may personally disapprove of abortion for "soft" reasons, but think that the decision should be a private one.

Increasing Incidence of Legal Abortion

The basis for legal termination of pregnancy had been expanded in 17 states between 1967 and 1972. In response to these legal changes and their often liberal interpretation, the incidence of legal abortion in the U.S. has skyrocketed over recent years from an estimated 6,000 in 1966 to over 200,000 in 1970 and probably over 500,000 in 1971 (Tietze, 1973a; U.S. Dept. of H.E.W., 1971). For the United States as a whole, the abortion ratio in 1971 was about 140 per 1,000 live births, indicating that roughly one out of every eight pregnancies was legally terminated by abortion. (It should be noted that the inclusion of illegal abortions in this ratio would make the ratio of abortions to births even higher. However, we do not have reliable data on illegal abortion.)

Although legal abortions increased in a number of states, and will be much more available as a result of the 1973 Supreme Court decision, New York and California accounted for almost 80 percent of the national total in 1971. New York City alone reported almost half of the 1971 abortions nationwide (U.S. Dept. of H.E.W., 1971). Since data for New York City are the most detailed and most complete, it is useful to focus on the experience of that city. In July 1970, abortion on demand became legal in New York for women less than 24 weeks pregnant.

During the first 24 months under the new law, an estimated 402,000 legal abortions were performed in New York City (Health Services Administration, 1972c). Even though nonresidents accounted for over two-thirds of the abortions in New York City, among residents of the city the abortion ratio (abortions per 1,000 births) was about 508 during 1971. Thus, among residents of New York City, roughly one of every three pregnancies was terminated by legal abortion (Health Services Administration, 1972a).

Although women in their early twenties account for the largest proportion of the abortions, significant numbers were either under 17 (11 percent) or over 35 (8 percent). Age at the time of abortion tended to be older among residents than among nonresidents. In 1971, one-third of the nonresidents were under 20 at the time of abortion, as compared with one-sixth of the residents. First pregnancies accounted for about two-fifths of the abortions to New York City residents and almost two-thirds of the abortions to nonresidents (Health Services Administration, 1972b).

The proportion of first-trimester abortions has continued to grow: over four-fifths of all abortions in New York City in late 1971 were performed within the first three months of pregnancy. Associated with this earlier timing has been an increase in the frequency of suction curettage, which is now used in roughly two-thirds of all New York City abortions (Health Services Administration, 1972b). As a consequence of these trends, complication rates have declined from 8.5 per 1,000 abortions in the first year of the law to 6.3 per 1,000 in 1971. Likewise, the rate of abortion deaths has declined from a rate of 4.2 per 100,000 abortions in the first year to the remarkably low rate of 3.5 deaths per 100,000 abortions in the second year. (Health Services Administration, 1972c and 1972d).

Demographic Implications of Increasing Legal Abortion

The consequences of the increasing practice of legal abortion are twofold. On the one hand, there is a very significant reduction in complications and mortality from illegal abortions. On the other hand, the legality of abortion undoubtedly results in the termination of many unwanted pregnancies that would not have been ended otherwise. The termination of these pregnancies is a net increment to the total number of abortions (legal and illegal) and, as such, has demographic consequences.

However, the demographic effects of abortion depend on the extent to which aborted pregnancies would have resulted in births that were not wanted until later (timing failures) or in births that were not wanted at all (number failures). Family size clearly is reduced by abortion of pregnancies that are number failures. However, the termination of pregnancies that are timing failures may also lead to smaller families—partly because of the reduction in fecundity that comes with age and partly because of the decrease in desired family size that a woman is likely to experience when she postpones motherhood (Presser, 1971). Since a high proportion of abortions occur among women with a low number of children, it is reasonable to suppose that a high proportion are timing-failure pregnancies.

Christopher Tietze has prepared estimates of the health and demographic impacts of legalized abortions to residents of New York City between July 1970 and July 1972 (Tietze, 1973b). He concludes that about 70 percent of the legal abortions during this time period were drawn from the illegal market. Declines in the maternal mortality rate (heavily influenced by deaths related to illegal abortions) strongly reflect this change. In 1971, this rate reached an all-time low of 29 deaths per 100,000 live births, compared with 53 in 1969, and 46 in 1970. The infant mortality rate has also reached a new low (Health Services Administration, 1972b).

That many of the legal abortions would not have been performed otherwise is reflected by the fact that illegitimate births declined in New York City in 1971 for the first time since 1954. Even the estimated 30 percent of New York City's legal abortions that were not drawn from the illegal market appear to have had a dramatic effect on the city's birthrate. This rate declined 23 percent between 1970 and 1972, about three times the nationwide decline. Tietze's estimates suggest that about 50 percent of this decline may be the result of legalization of abortion. Much of this decline may represent the short-run impact of people who have chosen to delay first births. However, much also represents direct and indirect reductions of total family size and hence has significant implications for the growth of the U.S. population.

CONCLUSION

During a period of growing expectations for complete fertility control, both sterilization and abortion have gained wider social approval and have become increasingly more prevalent. It is likely that both of these trends, especially in view of the Supreme Court decision, are only in their early stages and that the long-run implications of this revolution in fertility control in the U.S. (including the pill and the IUD) are phenomenal, not simply in terms of substantial reductions in births and population growth, but also in terms of the health and welfare of millions of American families.

REFERENCES

AMERICAN COLLEGE OF OBSTETRICIANS AND GYNECOLOGISTS. 1965. "Standards for Obstetric-Gynecologic Hospital Services." Merril, Mich.: American College.

BLAKE, JUDITH. 1971. "Abortion and Public Opinion: The 1960–1970 Decade." In *Science,* Vol. 171 (1971), pp. 540–549.

EISNER, THOMAS; VAN TIENHOVEN, ARI; & ROSENBLATT, FRANK. 1970. "Population Control, Sterilization, and Ignorance." In *Science,* Vol. 167 (1970), p. 337.

HEALTH SERVICES ADMINISTRATION, CITY OF NEW YORK DEPARTMENT OF HEALTH. 1972a. "Bulletin on Abortion Program: April 1972." New York.

———. 1972b. "News Release of Sunday, February 20." New York.

———. 1972c. "New York City Abortion Report, The First Two Years: October 1972." New York.

———. 1972d. "News Release of Tuesday, April 25." New York.

JONES, ELISE F., & WESTOFF, CHARLES F. 1973. "Attitudes Toward Abortion in the United States in 1970 and the Trend Since 1965." In *Demographic and Social Aspects of Population Growth,* Charles F. Westoff & Robert Parke, Jr., eds. Research Reports of the Commission on Population Growth and the American Future, Vol. 1. Washington: U.S. Government Printing Office.

PHILLIPS, NANCY. 1971. "The Prevalence of Surgical Sterilization in Suburban Populations." In *Demography,* Vol. 8 (1971), pp. 261–270.

PRESSER, HARRIET B. 1971. "The Timing of the First Birth, Female Roles, and Black Fertility." In *Milbank Memorial Fund Quarterly,* Vol. 49 (1971), pp. 329–361.

———. In press. "Sterilization and Fertility Decline in Puerto Rico." In *Population Monograph.* Berkeley, Calif.: University of California Press.

PRESSER, HARRIET B., & BUMPASS, LARRY L. 1973. "Demographic and Social Aspects of Contraceptive Sterilization in the United States: 1965–1970." In *Demographic and Social Aspects of Population Growth,* Charles F. Westoff & Robert Parke, Jr., eds. Research Reports of the Commission on Population Growth and the American Future, Vol. 1. Washington: U.S. Government Printing Office.

RYDER, NORMAN B., & WESTOFF, CHARLES F. 1971. *Reproduction in the U.S.: 1965.* Princeton, N.J.: Princeton University Press.

TIETZE, CHRISTOPHER. 1973a. "The Potential Impact of Legal Abortion on Population Growth in the United States." In *Demographic and Social Aspects of Population Growth,* Charles F. Westoff & Robert Parke, Jr., eds. Research Reports of the Commission on Population Growth and the American Future, Vol. 1. Washington: U.S. Government Printing Office.

———. 1973b. "Two Years' Experience with a Liberal Abortion Law: Its Impact on Fertility Trends in New York City." In *Family Planning,* Vol. 5 (1973), pp. 36–41.

U.S. DEPARTMENT OF HEALTH, EDUCATION AND WELFARE; PUBLIC HEALTH SERVICE, HEALTH SERVICES AND MENTAL HEALTH ADMINISTRATION. 1971. "Estimated Number of Legal Abortions Performed in the United States, July 1970–June 1971." Memorandum dated December 23, 1971.

WESTOFF, CHARLES F. 1972. "The Modernization of U.S. Contraceptive Practice." In *Family Planning Perspectives,* Vol. 4 (1972), pp. 9–12.

S. BRUCE SCHEARER ═══════════════════════════

5. *Tomorrow's Contraception*

EXPECTATIONS

Most people who use contraceptives look forward eagerly to the day when new and improved methods of fertility control will be available. The inconvenience, side-effects, and in some settings, costs of presently available contraceptive methods give rise to much dissatisfaction, and a significant share of the world's unwanted pregnancies stem from these disadvantages. Consequently, strong demands are placed on today's biomedical researchers, who have already demonstrated the capacity of their technology by breaking the genetic code, by creating "miracle" grains, and by unravelling much of the complex biology of human reproduction.

In recent years, increased funds and manpower have been committed to contraceptive development. Work on new contraceptive methods, once carried out only by pharmaceutical companies, is now being vigorously pursued under research and development projects sponsored by international agencies, national governments, universities, and foundations throughout the world. In addition to drug company expenditures, approximately $27 million was committed directly to the development of new contraceptive methods in the U.S. during

S. Bruce Schearer is a staff scientist in the Biomedical Division of The Population Council at Rockefeller University.

fiscal 1971 (U.S. Department of Health, Education, and Welfare, 1972; Population Council, 1973; World Health Organization, 1972). How successful have these efforts been? What is their prognosis? What lines of attack have they pursued? What products can users hope to gain in the foreseeable future?

To date, contraceptive development programs have identified about three dozen new leads (Population Council, 1973; World Health Organization, 1972; Corfman, 1971). Some of these involve direct improvements of current methods, such as more effective spermicides. Others, such as injectable contraceptives, are based on new modes of drug delivery to effect hormonal contraception like that now provided by the pill. Still others, such as medicated intrauterine devices, seek to exploit new biological principles. A few of the new leads are in the final stages of clinical testing and evaluation, and some should reach the public in the near future. Most are in earlier stages of clinical evaluation and will require from three to ten years for complete development and assessment. Still others have only recently entered clinical research trials or continue to be investigated in animals; most of these very early leads are probably more than 10 years away from general use. Of course, many of these leads will never appear on the shelves of drugstores and family planning clinics, and no one can be sure how soon they will be available or how many of them will ultimately prove useful. A good odds-maker would probably give no more than a 1-in-10 chance for the successful realization of any of the near-term leads, a 1-in-100 chance for the more distant ones.

NEW IUDs

Among the next generation of contraceptive methods (those farthest advanced in development and testing) are two new types of intrauterine devices. These devices improve upon an historically old method of contraception that is currently very popular. It is now known that any foreign body in the uterine cavity provokes an infiltration of white blood cells into the area, creating an environment that is inhospitable to both sperm and ovum. This leucocytic response, possibly combined with several other localized effects of the IUD, is thought to be responsible for its antifertility action. The newest devices are made of materials that have not previously been used in IUDs. One device that is now undergoing large-scale clinical testing is a Lippes Loop made of a special blended polymer instead of the standard polyethylene. Two other devices utilize copper attached to a polyethylene backbone. The copper is continuously eroded from the IUD into the uterus, where it acts as an antifertility agent until most of it is washed out with the monthly menses (Tatum, 1972). The advantages of these new devices are that they reduce the amount of bleeding and pain sometimes associated with intrauterine contraception and increase the level of contraceptive effectiveness nearly to that of the pill.

Considerably behind these new IUD models are a variety of medicated IUDs, which release extremely small amounts of antifertility drugs within the uterus. As yet, we have too little data to be able to judge how promising this intriguing approach may be.

LOW- AND MINI-DOSE ORAL CONTRACEPTIVES

Several new hormonal methods are also either near to or upon the public doorstep. All of these methods take advantage of estrogens and progesterone-like compounds called progestins, the two types of steroid hormones that are responsible for the contraceptive action of the pill. One approach now reaching the market employs these potent agents in lower doses, thus reducing many of the side-effects associated with the standard oral preparations (Preston, 1972). These combined low-dose orals, however, yield a higher incidence of menstrual irregularities and a slightly reduced protection against pregnancy. Many users are willing to accept these drawbacks in return for reduced side-effects. Recent visitors report that the massive Chinese family-planning program makes extensive use of three versions of the low-dose oral. Called the Shanghai I Pill, the Shanghai II Pill, and the Peking Pill, these formulations are the products of an active contraceptive development program in China (Faundes & Luukkainen, 1972).

Another hormonal method, also oral, has been developed merely by lowering the dose of the progestin component still further and dropping the estrogen completely. Called the mini-pill or micro-dose oral contraceptive (Laurie & Korba, 1972; Board, 1971), this approach has undergone widespread testing throughout the world and has very recently been marketed in several forms in the U.S. Unlike the low-dose orals, the mini-pill does not simply represent a modification of existing oral contraceptives. In a woman using the standard oral contraceptives, monthly ovulation is completely blocked and an artificial menstrual pattern is created by the combined effects of the two contraceptive steroids. The mini-pill, however, interrupts a different link (or set of links) in the chain of biological processes associated with reproduction. Ovulation occurs normally in most users, and menses is natural. Antifertility action is provided either by an alteration in the speed with which the egg is transported through the fallopian tubes from the ovary to the uterus, or by a change in the mucus of the cervix that impedes the passage of sperm, or by some other, thus far unknown effect on the female reproductive tract. Although still very effective, the mini-pill sacrifices some of the contraceptive efficacy of the standard orals in return for a much lower incidence of almost all side-effects. Menstrual irregularities, however, such as intermenstrual bleeding, spotting, or the missing of menstrual periods, occur more frequently.

LONG-ACTING METHODS

Several new drug delivery mechanisms would eliminate the disadvantage of daily pills. Among those currently undergoing clinical testing are once-a-month and longer-acting injectable contraceptives (Faundes & Luukkainen, 1972; Vecchio, 1972), both of which function like the standard oral contraceptives by suppressing ovulation. Since these methods do not artificially regulate menstruation, prospective users will have to choose between daily pill-taking with relatively normal cycles and infrequent injections with some menstrual irregularity. Some injectable contraceptives are now being marketed in other parts of the world, and women in the U.S. can expect to be offered an injectable product within the next several years.

A weekly pill that is now being clinically investigated will offer the same sort of choice. Much closer to marketing within the U.S. is a combined monthly pill that provides the user with a month's supply of estrogen and progestin in a single dose (Lotvin & Berman, 1970). In clinical trials in this country and in South America the monthly pill has proved to be about as effective as an IUD in preventing pregnancy. It does not control menstrual patterns as well as the daily pill, especially during the initial four or five months of use when a high incidence of menstrual irregularity occurs. But, in addition to its advantage as a once-a-month method, this pill exposes women to a significantly lower amount of the two contraceptive steroids. This monthly pill is now commercially available in some Latin American countries.

Two other clinically promising hormonal methods (Population Council, 1973) use novel drug-delivery systems. The first, one which acts by hormonal suppression, utilizes a doughnut-shaped ring placed in the vagina in the same position as a diaphragm. The ring, which releases a progestin contraceptive steroid through the vaginal tissues into the bloodstream, is left in place for about 20 days and then removed. A few days later an artificially induced menstruation occurs, after which the ring is reinserted by the user and the next cycle begins.

In the limited clinical trials that have been conducted thus far, this ingenious device appears to be well tolerated by users and by their partners as well. The second method acts through a mini-pill effect. It employs the same drug-releasing polymer, a silicone derivative, in a different form and with a much smaller amount of progestin. The steroid-containing polymer, designed as a small capsule, is implanted under the skin. A mini-dose of steroid is released continuously and contraceptive effectiveness is maintained for longer than one year. The mini-dose action of these subdermal implants promises the same assets and drawbacks as the oral mini-pill approach, but it confers protection that is both long-term and reversible. Both the vaginal ring and the implants could gain general use within 3 to 5 years.

POSTCOITAL AND PREOVULATORY APPROACHES

Several other promising hormonal contraceptives seek to exploit previously unattacked links in both the male and female reproductive system. For some time, gynecologists at a number of colleges have occasionally prescribed a potent estrogen as a postcoital pill for students who had ignored basic biology the night before (Kuchera, 1971). The hormonal basis of action of this treatment is being studied to determine whether pregnancy is blocked prior to or at the time of fertilization, at the point of implantation of the fertilized egg in the uterus, or subsequently as a result of decreased levels of the maternal hormone which normally supports pregnancy. A variety of new drugs are being clinically tested in an effort to identify a compound that will be effective without the severe gastrointestinal side-effects of the estrogen regimen. Since the underlying biology of this contraceptive approach is now fairly well understood, it is likely that a hormonal substance will be found to provide a suitable method for use on infrequent occasions when unprotected coitus has occurred.

A much more distant but much more tantalizing set of leads have surfaced quite recently, thanks to a major breakthrough in basic research in reproduction. It has been known for decades that the pituitary gland at the base of the brain oversees and coordinates the sex hormones of men and women. The new knowledge indicates that the pituitary itself is hormonally controlled by a nearby portion of the brain called the hypothalamus. The hypothalamus appears to act both metaphorically and biologically as the nerve center of reproduction, exerting its directing role by secreting a special set of hormones. These hormones, called releasing factors, are currently the subject of intensive investigation; several have recently been synthesized and are being used clinically. Plans have been formulated to use these releasing factor hormones in two ways to achieve contraception: either to block ovulation altogether or to cause ovulation to take place at a specific, known time during the menstrual cycle. If these plans work, a preovulatory method that is low in side-effects could become part of the contraceptive arsenal. Even with the best of fortune, however, it is likely that 5 to 10 years will be required for full development of such a method.

A MALE PILL

Another new approach has generated high anticipation both in and out of the contraceptive development field because it will be the first modern contraceptive method for the male. Since the advent of the combined oral contraceptive for women, researchers have attempted unsuccessfully to make use of parallel biological principles to inhibit sperm production in men. Since there is no need to regulate menstrual patterns, the job of developing a male pill would seem to be considerably easier.

In earlier research, the contraceptive steroids that suppress ovulation in the female were used to block spermatogenesis in males. It was found, however, that the males' testosterone levels dropped to near zero, with the result that sex drive virtually disappeared. Testosterone itself could not be administered orally to replenish the body's supply, because it fails to survive the digestive enzymes of the gastrointestinal tract. Very recently, however, new drug-delivery systems and more sensitive methods for measuring testosterone in the blood have led to a technique for circumventing the stomach and maintaining normal blood testosterone levels even when spermatogenesis is being repressed with contraceptive steroids (Segal, 1972). This new development has radically altered previous estimates on when a male method might become available. If the early promise of this new approach is borne out, the onus of contraception could be more equally distributed between women and men as soon as the late 1970s.

MENSES INDUCTION

Perhaps more thought has been devoted to approaches for inducing the flow of reluctant menses than to any other topic in contraceptive development. Referred to by some as the monthly pill, by others as abortifacients, two variations of the method are under development. Both differ fundamentally from the hormonal once-a-month pill described earlier because they act at the end of the cycle after pregnancy has been established. In one, a drug is administered just prior to menstruation to assure its appearance, whether or not conception has taken place. The other approach seeks to induce menstruation chemically after a period has been missed, either on the assumption or with a positive indication that pregnancy is responsible for the delay. A wide variety of chemical substances have been screened in animals and scores of these have subsequently undergone clinical testing, none with any real success. Although contraceptive steroids taken in the last part of the menstrual cycle do exhibit abortifacient-like activity, a significant number of the women tested fail to menstruate and continue their pregnancies without interruption (Nygren et al., 1972). The recent rediscovery of substances called prostaglandins fanned hopes in this field, because it was found that they could induce menstruation in patients with confirmed pregnancies. Further study, however, revealed that many of the abortions induced by prostaglandins are incomplete and that most women treated with these substances react with violent gastrointestinal side-effects (Bergstrom et al., 1972). Although these disappointments have been repeated in clinical trials with a wide variety of other compounds, vigorous research in this area continues. The appeal and utility of contraception by a monthly induction of menstruation guarantees that these efforts will continue in spite of current discouragement.

REVERSIBLE VASECTOMY

At present, men who seek to reverse a vasectomy have about a 60 percent chance of recovering their fertility (Presser, 1970). A good deal of effort is now being made to develop a procedure that would assure a 90 to 95 percent reversibility rate, thus making male sterilization a much more attractive alternative to families wishing to control their fertility. These efforts have centered around finding reversible methods of occluding instead of cutting of the vas deferens. In principle, any mechanism for plugging or simply clamping shut the vas would provide infertility by blocking the release of sperm into the ejaculate, while at the same time permit easy reversibility. But preliminary studies with silicone plugs, silk threads, valves, clips, and similar devices have demonstrated that living tissue is considerably more complex than inert tubing. In all of the clinical trials to date, the vas deferens in a significant number of men either managed to move away from the occluding substance, thus opening a passageway for the sperm, or underwent local inflammation that closed the vas permanently. Investigation continues in many centers around the world and, in spite of the setbacks to date, it seems highly likely that in the next few years a vas occlusion method providing about 90 percent reversibility will be introduced for general use.

PERMANENT METHODS OF FERTILITY CONTROL

Among the methods of fertility control currently available in the U.S., sterilization now ranks as the second most popular (see Chapter 3). Roughly half of all procedures are carried out on women and, until recently, they required hospitalization and major surgery. A variety of new female sterilization techniques are now being investigated, with the aim of developing a simple, out-patient procedure. One line of research is pursuing the use of highly sophisticated new instruments that make it possible to perform tubal ligations through a small puncture in the abdomen (laparoscopy) or vagina (culdoscopy). These methods are being widely tested in the U.S. and abroad and they will undoubtedly make sterilization a much simpler and less costly procedure for many women in the very near future (Richart & Prager, 1972).

A second line of research seeks to simplify sterilization by using nonsurgical procedures. Application of a caustic substance to the fallopian tubes by way of the vagina and cervix can be easily achieved in a gynecologist's office, with almost no side-effects. The resulting inflammation and the formation of scar tissue in the tubes blocks the future transport of eggs, thus providing permanent infertility. This approach has been used with close to a 90 percent success rate in preliminary trials in Chile (Zipper et al., in Richart & Prager, 1972), but much more extensive and longer-term clinical testing will be needed to demonstrate its ultimate value.

A third approach to both male and female sterilization attacks the problem in a totally different way—through immunization against pregnancy. Of all of today's leads, the contraceptive vaccine has the best potential to serve as the "ideal" method of fertility control for people who choose never to have more children (and possibly even those interested in greater spacing of births). Of all of the leads, however, it is also the furthest from development, for it has only recently entered the earliest stages of clinical testing.

A PREDICTOR'S PREDICTION

It is safe to predict that however many of the current contraceptive leads clear the hurdles of testing and development, none will be altogether free of drawbacks. Each new method will offer the user at best a slight, but significant improvement over existing methods, at worst a chance to choose one set of disadvantages in place of another. The truly ideal contraceptive—one that is completely effective yet reversible, free of all side-effects, unconnected with the sexual act, and convenient to use—has not yet appeared on tomorrow's horizon.

Nonetheless, knowledge of many of the biological principles that underlie human reproduction clearly indicates that near-to-ideal methods are feasible. There can be no doubt that the amount of time required to develop them will depend directly on the amount of scientific manpower and resources devoted to this effort.

REFERENCES

BERGSTROM, S.; GREEN, K.; & SAMUELSSON, B. (eds.). 1972. *Prostaglandins in Fertility Control.* Stockholm: World Health Organization Research and Training Centre on Human Reproduction, Karolinska Institutet.

BOARD, J. A. 1971. "Continuous Norethindrone, 0.35 mg, As an Oral Contraceptive Agent." In *American Journal of Obstetrics and Gynecology,* Vol. 109 (1971), p. 531.

CORFMAN, P. A. 1971. "A Five-Year Plan for Population Research and Family Planning Services." In *Family Planning Perspectives,* Vol. 3, no. 4 (1971), p. 41.

FAUNDES, A., & LUUKKAINEN, T. 1972. "Health and Family Planning Services in the Chinese People's Republic." In *Studies in Family Planning,* Vol. 3, no. 7 (1972), Supplement.

KUCHERA, L. K. 1971. "Postcoital Contraception with Diethylstilbestrol." In *Journal of the American Medical Association,* Vol. 218 (1971), p. 562.

LAURIE, R. E., & KORBA, V. D. 1972. "Fertility Control with Continuous Microdose Norgestrel." In *Journal of Reproductive Medicine,* Vol. 8 (1972), p. 165.

LOTVIN, B. R., & BERMAN, E. 1970. "Once-a-Month Oral Contraceptive: Quinestrol and Quinestanol." In *Obstetrics and Gynecology,* Vol. 35 (1970), p. 933.

NYGREN, K.; JOHANSSON, E. D. B.; & WIDE, L. 1972. "Postovulatory Contraception in Women with Large Doses of Norethindrone." In *Contraception,* Vol. 5 (1972), p. 445.

The Population Council Annual Report 1972. New York: The Population Council, 1973.

PRESSER, H. B. 1970. "Voluntary Sterilization: A World View." In *Reports on Population/Family Planning,* no. 5 (1970).

PRESTON, S. N. 1972. "A Report of a Collaborative Dose-Response Clinical Study Using Decreasing Doses of Combination Oral Contraceptives." In *Contraception,* Vol. 6 (1972), p. 17.

RICHART, R. M., & PRAEGER, D. J. (eds.). 1972. *Human Sterilization.* Springfield, Ill.: Charles C. Thomas.

SEGAL, S. J. 1972. "Contraceptive Research: A Male Chauvinist Plot?" In *Family Planning Perspectives,* Vol. 4, no. 3 (1972), p. 21.

TATUM, H. J. 1972. "Intrauterine Contraception." In *American Journal of Obstetrics and Gynecology,* Vol. 112 (1972), p. 1000.

VECCHIO, T. J. 1972. "Depo-Provera Contraception: International Experience in Over 20,000 Cases." In *Journal of Reproductive Medicine,* Vol. 8 (1972), p. 208.

U.S. DEPARTMENT OF HEALTH, EDUCATION AND WELFARE. 1972. *Population Research: the federal program.* DHEW Publication No. (NIH 72–133), p. 7.

WORLD HEALTH ORGANIZATION. 1972. *Expanded Programme of Research Development and Research Training in Human Reproduction: Program Strategy and Implementation.* Geneva: World Health Organization.

NORMAN B. RYDER ══════════════════════════════

6. Recent Trends and Group Differences in Fertility

The changes in American fertility patterns in the twentieth century are simpler to describe than they are to explain. No matter what index we choose, we see a decline to a trough during the 1930s, a rise to a moderately high plateau during the 1950s, and a decline since then. It is not surprising that the general direction of change during this century has been downward, since the same was true of the entire preceding century. The conventional explanation of the nineteenth-century decline—that it was part of a major process of social change that included industrialization, urbanization, and modernization—still remains broadly viable. What was unanimously unpredicted and remains unexplained was that high postwar plateau known familiarly as the "baby boom." An explanation of that phenomenon is essential if we are to understand what has happened since.

In the first section of this chapter, we sketch the major changes in American fertility during the past 50 years. Next, we suggest some influential factors in the evolution of the current fertility pattern that have previously been neglected. The third section contains a discus-

Norman B. Ryder is a professor of sociology and a faculty associate of the Office of Population Research at Princeton University. Most of his previous professional career was spent on the faculty of the University of Wisconsin. He has concentrated on methodological aspects of demography and studies of American fertility. He has just completed a term as president of the Population Association of America.

sion of some sociocultural variations from the national average. Finally we bring some up-to-date evidence to bear on the contemporary collapse of the birthrate.

CHANGES IN AMERICAN FERTILITY

The best measure of fertility is obtained by cumulating the reproductive performance of women age by age, as they pass through their reproductive years, and then calculating the average number of births per woman. (Demographers call this the "cohort* total fertility rate.") The result of this calculation for the United States, over the past 50 years, is shown in the solid line in Figure 6-1. Two comments may make this time series a little more understandable. First, we have assigned a date to each total fertility rate (TFR) to correspond with the time when the women concerned were at their central childbearing age (which is around age 26). Second, we have had to make estimates for the more recent experience because demographers do not know any more than the women involved how many children they will end up with.

Figure 6-1 also shows a broken line, which represents the time series of the average age of childbearing. This is an interesting piece of information in its own right, but it has a special significance as well. Whenever the average age of childbearing (called the "mean age of cohort fertility") is rising—as it was during the Depression and as it is now—the yearly records of fertility are going to be distorted below their normal level, because a tendency to have children at later ages is tantamount to spreading out reproductive performance more thinly over the years involved. Thus we should not take too literally the low level of the current birth rate, since it is caused partly by a rise in the age of childbearing. Conversely, a decline in the average age of childbearing, such as the one that occurred between the end of World War II and the early 1960s, causes fertility to be buoyed up artificially, because the amount of childbearing going on is packed more tightly into each year of observation.

What we see in Figure 6-1 is that the average number of births per woman dropped to a minimum of nearly 2.2 during the Depression years, accompanying a rise in the average age of childbearing (associated with postponement), and then rose to a peak of 3.3 during the

* A cohort is an aggregate of persons with a common time of occurrence of a significant event in their personal history. The concept most frequently refers to a birth cohort. Thus here we mean by cohort all women born during some specified time period.

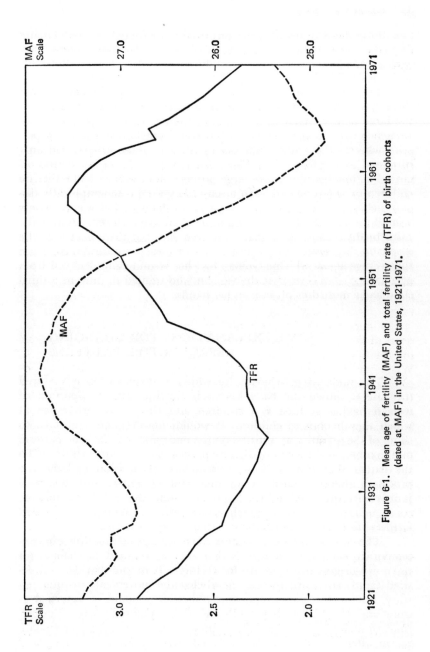

Figure 6-1. Mean age of fertility (MAF) and total fertility rate (TFR) of birth cohorts (dated at MAF) in the United States, 1921-1971.

late 1950s. Since then the average number of births per woman has decreased, so that it is currently almost at the Depression minimum again, and the average age of childbearing, which had declined for such a long time, has reversed itself and started to rise again.

The rise in fertility shown in Figure 6-1 during the period from the 1930s to the 1950s should not be taken as evidence of a return of the large family. What actually happened was that the proportion of women having at least two children rose from 55 percent to 85 percent, whereas the average number of children those women had only increased from 3.63 to 3.78. The low fertility of the earlier period occurred mainly because a very large proportion of women had either no children or only one child—in a sense they were demographically disenfranchised. The principal change in the later period was that only a small proportion of women had fewer than two children. Admittedly, third births became somewhat more frequent, but there is at least the suspicion that a substantial proportion of these were unwanted. Since the average age at which a woman had her second child declined from 27.2 to 24.7, it is clear that the woman who wanted to prevent a third child had a more difficult task on her hands.

SOME EXPLANATIONS FOR CHANGING REPRODUCTIVE PATTERNS

The underlying behavior for which an explanation is required (because it caused the baby boom) is the increasing proportion of women having at least two children and the much earlier age at which they had those children. It would, however, be a mistake to think of the quantity of fertility, on the one hand, and its time pattern, on the other, as if they were discrete parts of some lifetime strategy. To the extent that fertility is a consequence of decision making, the process is almost certainly conditional and sequential, and concerned jointly with quantity and time. To the extent that fertility is not the consequence of decision so much as of error, the quantity of unwanted fertility varies directly with the length of exposure to risk.

The conventional explanation of the swings up and down in contemporary American fertility is that they correspond to changes (of unknown origin) in the desire for children. It is true that data on desired family size have roughly paralleled the movements in total fertility, but we think it a moot question which should be regarded as cause and which effect. It would seem at least plausible that such questions would yield a compound of fantasy before the fact and rationalization after the fact. In the National Fertility Studies of 1965 and

1970, we have attempted to have respondents classify each of their pregnancies in turn as wanted or unwanted, in terms of their intentions prior to conception (Ryder & Westoff, 1973). The answers reveal a great deal of unwanted fertility in the 1950s, despite the stated levels of desired family size. We are, however, skeptical that we have succeeded in estimating the true magnitude of unwanted births. The problem is that respondents are being asked to confess their inability to control a crucial dimension of their lives and at the same time to deny the legitimacy of the existence of one of their children.

Our own view is that the course of American fertility in the twentieth century can be explained by a fixed set of reproductive norms operating within a changing context. These norms specify that all people are expected to marry and have two children as soon as, and providing that, their economic circumstances permit. The economic constraint is couched in terms of the scale of living to which they aspire. The critical variable for explanation is the age at which parenthood begins and the fundamental determinant of that is the labor market for young adults. The receptivity of the labor market to each entering cohort depends on the supply of that cohort (its numbers) relative to the demand for its services (the state of the economy).

In the 1930s, it took much longer to fulfill the conditions for beginning reproduction than it did in the 1950s. During the Depression, the supply of young adults was large and the demand apparently small; in the 1950s the situation was reversed. Furthermore, the frame of reference for young adults in the 1930s was the relatively prosperous previous era in which they were raised; the converse was true of their counterparts during the postwar period. Another dimension to cohort size may be relevant: membership in a large cohort implies that the help available from one's parents must be shared with more siblings; the cohort of small size does not share this comparative disadvantage.

Many social and demographic consequences result from the age at which childbearing begins. An early beginning reduces the length of the wife's exposure to the attractions of nondomestic life. She is still young when the second child arrives and has had little experience with the labor market. Thus the alternative opportunity cost of yet another child may be viewed as small. If economic pressures are insufficient to make it important to prevent a third child, the couple may become ambivalent about its desirability and relax their contraceptive vigilance. Perhaps most important, an early beginning implies early and long exposure to the risk of unwanted fertility. A late beginning to childbearing, on the other hand, promotes lower fertility, partly for physiological reasons, partly because of the perception of declining capacity to cope with childbearing, partly because nonparental interests have an opportunity to develop during the postponement period, and partly because the ability to prevent an unwanted child increases with the passage of time, that is, the time gained by successful postponement.

The thesis we have advanced concerning the determinants of fertility, while accurate on the whole, does nonetheless neglect the substantial departure of various subcultures from the norms. These variations are the subject of the following section.

SOCIOCULTURAL VARIANCE IN FERTILITY

We now turn our attention to variance in reproductive patterns along various sociocultural dimensions. Table 6-1 illustrates two important categories of fertility differential, by race and by education. Looking first at the 1961–1965 data, and focusing our attention on total births, we see that black fertility exceeded white fertility by some 40 percent. For the total sample, and for the races separately, fertility was inversely correlated with education. The division of total births into wanted and unwanted births shows that the level of wanted fertility was not different between whites and blacks, and varied directly (albeit weakly) with education, at least among whites. The source of the differences in total births is unwanted fertility. Blacks had approximately three times as many unwanted births per capita as whites. The variation by years of schooling was strong and negative. These relationships represent fairly the kinds of differentials reported in previous national fertility surveys.

Looking now at the experience of 1966–1970, we find that the situation is very different. The excess of black over white fertility has shrunk to 10 percent. There is no longer a fertility differential by education for whites. The source of these changes is predominantly the unwanted component. On an education-specific basis, the levels of unwanted fertility for blacks in the later period correspond closely with those for whites in the earlier period. There are still differences in unwanted fertility between blacks and whites, and by education, but they have been sharply attenuated in the five-year interval.

Table 6-2 shows the proportion of respondents using one or the other of the two new and highly effective contraceptives—the pill and the intrauterine device. There has been a substantial increase in use of these methods in the period between the two studies, especially among blacks and among whites with low education, and this has undoubtedly been a major cause of the drop in unwanted fertility. (To gain some perspective on the proportions in Table 6-2, note that only two-thirds

TABLE 6–1.   MEAN NUMBER OF BIRTHS[a] PER MARRIED COUPLE
—TOTAL, WANTED, AND UNWANTED—1961–1965 AND
1966–1970 (BY RACE AND EDUCATION OF WIFE)

Education	1961-1965			1966-1970		
	Total[b]	White	Black	Total[b]	White	Black
	Total Births					
All levels	0.85	0.82	1.14	0.68	0.67	0.74
College	0.79	0.78	0.84	0.66	0.67	0.51
High school						
(4 years)	0.81	0.78	1.16	0.70	0.68	0.83
Less	0.94	0.89	1.18	0.69	0.65	0.77
	Wanted Births					
All levels	0.65	0.65	0.64	0.58	0.58	0.54
College	0.69	0.68	0.62	.0.60	.0.61	0.44
High school						
(4 years)	0.66	0.65	0.76	0.60	0.59	0.68
Less	0.62	0.63	0.58	0.53	0.53	0.48
	Unwanted Births					
All levels	0.20	0.16	0.49	0.10	0.09	0.20
College	0.10	0.10	0.22	0.06	0.06	0.07
High school						
(4 years)	0.15	0.13	0.40	0.10	0.09	0.16
Less	0.32	0.26	0.60	0.16	0.13	0.29

Source: 1965 and 1970 National Fertility Studies.

[a]"Births" include current pregnancies.

[b]"Total " includes other races.

of the group, at any point in time, would qualify as potential users of contraception, since the rest would be pregnant, trying to get pregnant, or sterile.) Whereas in 1965 the proportion of whites using the pill or the IUD was almost twice as high as that of blacks, the latter was the higher figure in 1970. As for differences in use by education, the lower the level in 1965, the larger the proportional increase by 1970.

TABLE 6-2. MARRIED WOMEN[a] USING EITHER PILL OR
IUD IN SEPTEMBER 1965 AND 1970
(BY RACE AND EDUCATION OF WIFE)

Education	1965			1970		
	Total	White	Black	Total	White	Black
All levels	28%	29%	15%	38%	38%	40%
College	34	35	21	42	41	45
High school (4 years)	27	29	14	39	38	41
Less	22	24	12	33	33	37

Source: 1970 National Fertility Study.
[a]Husband present, marital duration less than 10 years, age at marriage less than 25.

These new techniques, which by 1965 had diffused in a selective fashion to whites and those of higher education, have by 1970 permeated the entire social structure, and the consequences for future fertility patterns are considerable. It should also be emphasized that these two techniques do not represent the only areas of improvement in contraceptive effectiveness. There has been a pronounced increase in the use of sterilization among both males and by females. It is also likely that wider accessibility of legal abortions has decreased the probability that unwanted pregnancies will result in live births.

The other major category of differences in fertility in the United States has been religion. Within the white subpopulation, Catholic fertility has been substantially higher than that of non-Catholics in every national survey. For example, in the 1965 National Fertility Study, Catholics expected a total of 3.83 births, whereas non-Catholics expected 3.06. Elsewhere in that study we showed that, although Catholic efforts to prevent excess fertility were indeed less successful than those of non-Catholics, the predominant reason for higher Catholic fertility was that they wanted more children (Ryder & Westoff, 1971). From the 1970 National Fertility Study we note that, when cohort fertility was at its peak, the mean number of wanted births was 3.32 for Catholics and 2.55 for non-Catholics. For the most recent cohort, however, the values are 2.75 and 2.35 respectively, one-half the previous difference.

There has also been convergence in the ability to prevent unwanted fertility. We have presented elsewhere a measure of the rate of unwanted birth per thousand person-years of exposure to risk, for selected subsamples (Ryder & Westoff, 1973). Between the 1961–1965 period and the 1966–1970 period, the rate declined from 43 to 29 for non-Catholics and from 66 to 36 for Catholics. The difference has been reduced by more than one-half. One reason for convergence in effectiveness of fertility regulation comes from the proportions using the pill or the IUD. Between September 1965 and September 1970 the proportion rose from 33 percent to 40 percent for non-Catholics, and from 18 percent to 32 percent for Catholics. In summary, the differences between religious groups, like those between the races and educational levels, have diminished appreciably during the past decade for wanted fertility, for unwanted fertility, and for modes of fertility regulation.

A single framework encompasses most theories about the sources of differences in fertility. The transition from high to low fertility experienced by all modern countries is customarily explained by the transformation of the social structure implicit in industrialization, in brief, the movement from a traditional to a rational way of life. The same is true of fertility differences. The more the process of modernization has affected a group, the lower its fertility. Modernization enhances the importance of urban industry relative to rural agriculture, and the importance of the individual relative to the family. The child is transformed from a source of labor in the family enterprise to a consumer of education. Modern urban life releases the woman from bondage to the home. This process occurs sequentially through the social ranks, with those of higher status being the first to adopt the new ways and profit from them. The application of rationality in the reproductive sphere is highly correlated with its application elsewhere; each in turn depends on the extent to which there is confidence in future rewards for present effort.

High fertility can be expected in subpopulations where tradition and religion are important, because of their emphasis on the family vis-à-vis the individual, the father vis-à-vis the child, the husband vis-à-vis the wife, and the spiritual vis-à-vis the material world. These conditions are most likely in rural society. Yet it would be unwise to stress too much the economic exploitation of children and women in the premodern world. Children and family are alternatives to material success both as sources of satisfaction and as primitive social security systems.

Except for the committed Catholic, the high-fertility subpopulations have been the Southern blacks, the Southwest Mexican-Americans, the Appalachian whites, the Puerto Ricans, and the American Indians. All of these groups are poor, uneducated, and rural in origin. All belong to separate, isolated, highly visible minorities and all are excluded from the dominant culture and its resources, and thus from full participation in the process of modernization that produces low fertility. They lack the skills necessary to succeed in many areas of life, including the prevention of unwanted children. Perhaps a life of uncertainty and futility, reinforced by that other-worldly orientation that is the traditional consolation of the destitute and deprived, makes planning for the future seem a pointless exercise. Perhaps also the exclusion from the dominant subculture is accompanied by the development of subcultural norms that help reduce the cost of minority membership in the short run, but at the cost of reinforcing the boundaries and limitations imposed by the majority culture.

The case of the committed Catholic is somewhat different. Certainly some of the excess of Catholic over non-Catholic fertility has been the consequence of the Church's disapproval of all means of fertility regulation except the notoriously ineffective rhythm method, but this explanation bypasses the point that Catholics have, at least until very recently, accepted this limitation on their exercise of reproductive rationality. Moreover, Catholics have always reported that they want more children than non-Catholics. Probably the predominant source of support for this desire for relatively more children, and of acquiescence to restrictions on effective fertility regulation, is the subcultural emphasis on family solidarity as the bedrock of the social order, as can also be seen in the strength of Catholic opposition to premarital contraception, to divorce, and to equality for women. The Catholic family, like the Catholic Church, retains a patriarchal structure. Commitment to spiritual values competes with the secular interests that would promote lower fertility. And, finally, the Catholic community provides consolation and reassurance for those who have more children than they can support.

The view of fertility differences presented here is essentially time-bound. The essence of the position is that groups that still have higher-than-average fertility have not yet become modern. The inference is that, as they come to participate more fully and equally in modern life, and as the secular values of primacy of the individual—particularly the child and the woman—permeate the entire social system, their fertility will also decline. The data presented in this section represent strong support for this thesis.

THE CURRENT DECLINE IN FERTILITY

Table 6-1 shows a 20 percent decline in the mean number of births per woman from 0.85 for 1961–1965 to 0.68 for 1966–1970. The vital statistics for all women in these two periods show a 24 percent decline in total fertility rate, from 3.3 to 2.5. (The difference between 20 percent and 24 percent decline can be explained by the fact that the former figure does not include unmarried women.) The Current Population Surveys conducted by the Bureau of the Census report that the proportion of women who are or have been married declined, between 1965 and 1971, by 15 percent for those aged 18–19, by 6 percent for those aged 20–24, and by 4 percent for those aged 25–29. This probably reflects a combination of less marriage and later marriage. Other data document a recent rise in the female age at first marriage.

The cohort series graphed in Figure 6-1 suggest that the cohort total fertility rate declined by 14 percent from 1961–1965 to 1966–1970 (from 3.01 to 2.58) and that the rest of the decline in period fertility resulted from a shift from positive distortion in 1961–1965 (the cohort mean age of fertility was declining) to negative distortion in 1966–1970 (the cohort mean age of fertility was rising). The point has important implications for our judgment about the extent to which the decline in marital fertility, reported in Table 6-1, is a consequence of lower wanted or of lower unwanted fertility, respectively. Although wanted fertility did decline by 10 percent between the two periods, this is a period measure, which is therefore responsive to the influences of positive and negative distortion. If, as seems highly likely, there was a shift during the decade from declining to rising mean age of wanted fertility, then the observed decline in the level of wanted fertility could at least in part be explained by a change in distortion. Wanted fertility, cohort by cohort, may not have changed. The following circumstance makes that interpretation even more plausible: we know from vital statistics data that the mean age of fertility was rising during the late 1960s and that the rise can only partly be explained by an increase in the mean age at first marriage. We also know that the proportion of unwanted births was declining rapidly. On the assumption that unwanted births occur later in life than wanted births, we infer that the mean age of wanted fertility was rising even more than the mean age of total fertility. Our conclusion is that the level of wanted fertility, for cohorts, has probably changed little during the 1960s.

In summary, two circumstances of the last decade explain the decline in the birth rate: one is the rise in the mean age of wanted fertility; the other is the decline in unwanted fertility. The means by which these occurred was improved fertility regulation. The motivation can be explained in the same terms used in the discussion of the trough of the 1930s and the peak of the 1950s: young adults are currently larger cohorts in size, raised in comparative affluence, and facing at least temporarily lower demand for their services in the labor market.

The birthrate in the first nine months of 1972 was close to 15 per thousand per annum. The period total fertility was below 2.2 (as it was during the 1930s). Cohort fertility, although declining, was still some 10 percent above the replacement level of 2.11. The present low level of fertility may be a temporary aberration and we know that changes in the age distribution during the next decade will exert an upward pressure on the birth rate. Nevertheless, it is our judgment that stability, or even continued decline, in the birth rate is at least as likely as increase. This judgment is based on continuing increase in cohort size, the progressive removal of technical and legal impediments to all modes of fertility regulation—contraception, sterilization, and abortion —and a strong impression that some women are coming to perceive motherhood as a matter of choice rather than necessity.

Such a conclusion must be regarded with considerable doubt. The forecasting record of demographers has in the past been notoriously imperfect. Whatever happens in the future, however, it is clear that the patterns of reproduction and of fertility regulation—for the nation as a whole and for its subcultural components—are completely different from what they were only a decade ago. In this fundamental area of personal and family life, we have at last entered the modern era.

REFERENCES

RYDER, N. B., & WESTOFF, C. F. 1973. "Trend in Unwanted Fertility in the United States: 1965–1970." In *Demographic and Social Aspects of Population Growth,* Charles F. Westoff & Robert Parke, Jr., eds. Research Reports of the Commission on Population Growth and the American Future, Vol. I. Washington: U.S. Government Printing Office, pp. 467–87.

———. 1971. *Reproduction in the United States: 1965.* Princeton, N.J.: Princeton University Press.

7. U.S. Population Growth in International Perspective

This chapter will attempt to assess the past, present, and future levels of U.S. population growth in an international perspective. If such a broad topic is to be manageable, we must immediately impose a few restrictions. First, we shall not deal with all nations of the world, but only with the industrialized or developed nations, with which the U.S. can be most appropriately compared. Second, since the impact of changes in mortality conditions in the recent past and near future in these countries is relatively small when compared to changes in fertility levels, we shall concentrate almost entirely on U.S. fertility in international perspective. The most appropriate measure of fertility is the *total fertility rate,* which is defined as "the average number of live-born children that a woman would bear if she experienced current age-specific rates as she passed through her fertile period."

An important concept to keep in mind in the discussion that follows is the notion of *replacement fertility.* In general, replacement fertility means the level of fertility required to *replace* the reproducing generation, taking account of the small amount of mortality expected to occur before the newly born generation reaches reproductive age. Hence, replacement fertility would require a minimal average of one female birth per woman, or about 2.05 births per woman, since 1.05

Michael S. Teitelbaum, formerly at Oxford University, is currently an assistant professor of sociology and faculty associate at the Office of Population Research at Princeton University. He is specializing in demography and social biology.

TABLE 7-1. TOTAL FERTILITY RATES IN 26
INDUSTRIALIZED COUNTRIES: (1945-1970)

| | PATTERN I | | | | PATTERN III | |
Year	United States	Canada	Australia	New Zealand	Bulgaria	Czechos-lovakia
1945	2.49	3.02	2.75	2.92	—	—
1946	2.94	3.37	3.00	3.27		—
1947	3.27	3.60	3.06	3.46	2.97	3.10
1948	3.11	3.44	2.98	3.40		2.99
1949	3.11	3.46	3.00	3.34		2.89
1950	3.09	3.46	3.06	3.40		3.03
1951	3.27	3.50	3.06	3.38		3.02
1952	3.36	3.64	3.18	3.54	2.56	2.96
1953	3.42	3.72	3.20	3.50		2.87
1954	3.54	3.83	3.20	3.62		2.84
1955	3.58	3.83	3.27	3.74	2.41	2.85
1956	3.69	3.86	3.30	3.79	—	2.85
1957	3.77	3.92	3.41	3.90	2.29	2.75
1958	3.70	3.88	3.42	3.98	2.25	2.58
1959	3.71	3.94	3.45	4.02	2.25	2.39
1960	3.65	3.90	3.44	4.05	2.32	2.39
1961	3.63	3.84	3.54	4.18	2.28	2.39
1962	3.47	3.76	3.41	4.06	2.23	2.36
1963	3.33	3.67	3.34	3.82	2.21	2.51
1964	3.21	3.50	3.14	3.61	2.18	2.52
1965	2.93	3.14	2.97	3.34	2.07	2.38
1966	2.74	2.81	2.89^f	3.25	2.00	2.24
1967	2.57	2.59	2.86^f	3.22	2.01	2.09
1968	2.48	2.44	2.90^f	3.17	2.29	2.07
1969	2.45^a	2.39	2.89^f	3.13	—	2.04
1970	2.47^a	2.31	2.86^g	—	—	—
1971	2.28^b	2.19^d	2.95^g	—	—	—
(1972)	(2.04^c)	(2.09^e)	—	—		

Note: Total fertility rates "near" replacement level (defined as ≤2.25) are underlined. Total fertility rates at or below replacement level (defined as ≤2.11) are double-underlined.

^{a}Official estimates.

^{b}Unofficial estimates obtained by indirect standardization of latest available age-specific fertility rates (1968) on 1971 estimate of female population by age.

^{c}Estimated total fertility for first nine months of 1972. U.S. Department of Commerce, Bureau of the Census, Current Population Reports, Series P. 25, no. 493 (December 1972), p. 8, fn. 13.

TABLE 7-1 (cont.)

	PATTERN III (con't)						
Year	Hungary	Poland	Rumania	Yugo-slavia	East Germany	USSR	*Japan*
1945	—	—	—	—	—	—	—
1946	—	—	—	—	—	—	—
1947	—	} 3.29	—	—	—	—	4.52
1948	} 2.57		—	—	—	—	4.38
1949			—	4.13	—	—	4.29
1950	—	3.71	—	4.19	—	—	3.62
1951	—	3.74	—	4.24	—	—	3.25
1952	2.49	3.65	—	4.30	2.39	—	2.98
1953	2.76	3.62	—	3.38	2.36	—	2.69
1954	2.96	3.59	—	3.37	2.35	—	2.47
1955	2.79	3.61	3.07	3.17	2.34	—	2.36
1956	2.61	3.51	2.89	3.02	2.27	—	2.20
1957	2.28	3.49	2.73	2.77	2.11	2.84^h	2.03
1958	2.17	3.36	2.59	2.77	2.21	2.82^i	2.10
1959	2.08	3.20	2.43	2.72	2.35	—	2.03
1960	2.02	2.98	2.34	2.82	2.40	2.82^j	1.99
1961	1.94	2.82	2.17	2.75	—	—	1.95
1962	1.80	2.70	2.04	2.69	—	—	1.95
1963	1.82	2.70	2.01	2.68	2.47	2.52^k	1.98
1964	1.81	2.57	1.96	2.65	2.52	2.46^l	1.89
1965	1.81	2.52	1.91	2.72	2.47	2.46^m	2.14
1966	1.88	2.43	1.90	2.66	2.43	2.44^n	1.58
1967	2.01	2.33	3.66	2.60	2.34	2.41^o	2.22
1968	2.07	2.24	3.63	2.47^g	2.27^g	—	2.09^g
1969	2.03^g	—	3.19	2.43^g	—	—	2.07^g
1970	1.95^g	—	2.89	—	—	—	—
1971	1.89^g	2.25^g	—	—	—	—	—

dApproximation for 1971 calendar year estimated at the Office of Population Research from figure in Statistics Canada, Vol. 20, no. 6 (June 1972).

eOfficial estimate for 12-month period July 1, 1971, through June 30, 1972, Statistics Canada, Vol. 20, no. 6 (June 1972).

fOfficial Yearbook of the Commonwealth of Australia, no. 57 (1971), p. 161.

gUnofficial estimates calculated at the Office of Population Research from Office of Population Censuses and Surveys, The Registrar General's Quarterly Return for England and Wales, Quarter ended 30 June 1970.

h1957-58. i1958-59. j1960-61. k1963-64. l1964-65.
m1965-66. n1966-67. o1967-68.

TABLE 7-1 (cont.)

			PATTERN II			
Year	Denmark	Finland	Norway	West Germany	Belgium	Nether- lands
1945	2.97	3.04	2.43	—	<u>2.16</u>	2.95
1946	3.01	3.41	2.76	—	2.51	3.96
1947	2.89	3.47	2.64	<u><u>2.02</u></u>	2.45	3.69
1948	2.70	3.47	2.54	<u><u>2.07</u></u>	2.45	3.38
1949	2.58	3.32	2.49	<u>2.14</u>	2.39	3.22
1950	2.60	3.14	2.49	<u><u>2.09</u></u>	2.35	3.09
1951	2.50	3.02	2.43	<u><u>2.06</u></u>	2.29	3.15
1952	2.54	3.06	2.56	<u><u>2.08</u></u>	2.33	3.09
1953	2.58	2.95	2.64	<u><u>2.08</u></u>	2.33	3.03
1954	2.54	2.85	2.68	<u>2.13</u>	2.37	3.01
1955	2.57	2.93	2.74	<u>2.13</u>	2.39	3.06
1956	2.59	2.91	2.83	<u>2.23</u>	2.43	3.06
1957	2.55	2.86	2.82	2.32	2.47	3.08
1958	2.54	2.69	2.85	2.39	2.51	3.11
1959	2.50	2.75	2.86	2.40	2.59	3.18
1960	2.56	2.72	2.84	2.49	2.56	3.13
1961	2.56	2.70	2.87	2.44	2.64	3.23
1962	2.56	2.64	2.88	2.52	2.59	3.19
1963	2.66	2.64	2.92	2.52	2.68	3.20
1964	2.60	2.53	2.94	2.55	2.71	3.19
1965	2.61	2.40	2.91	2.51	2.61	3.04
1966	2.62	2.34	2.87	2.54	2.53	2.92
1967	2.36	<u>2.24</u>	2.80	2.49	2.42	2.82
1968	<u>2.12</u>	<u>2.07</u>	2.75	2.39	2.31	2.73
1969	<u><u>2.00</u></u>	<u>1.85</u>	2.70	2.22$	—	—

Note: Total fertility rates "near" replacement level (defined as ≤ 2.25) are underlined. Total fertility rates at or below replacement level (defined as ≤ 2.11) are double-underlined.

TABLE 7-1 (cont.)

				PATTERN II (con't)			
Year	Switzer-land	Austria	Italy	England & Wales	Scotland	France	Sweden
1945	2.61	—	2.32	2.04	2.24	2.29	2.60
1946	2.65		2.92	2.49	2.76	2.97	2.56
1947	2.61	2.30	2.84	2.70	3.09	3.01	2.50
1948	2.65		2.82	2.39	2.72	2.97	2.48
1949	2.59		2.61	2.26	2.61	2.97	2.37
1950	2.57	—	2.51	2.18	2.53	2.93	2.29
1951	2.49	2.03	2.36	2.16	2.41	2.77	2.21
1952	2.56	2.05	2.32	2.16	2.43	2.73	2.23
1953	2.56	2.07	2.30	2.22	2.43	2.66	2.27
1954	2.40	2.11	2.36	2.20	2.49	2.69	2.17
1955	2.27	2.22	2.36	2.22	2.53	2.68	2.25
1956	2.30	2.41	2.38	2.36	2.63	2.67	2.27
1957	2.35	2.47	2.32	2.45	2.73	2.70	2.29
1958	2.33	2.53	2.28	2.51	2.79	2.69	2.24
1959	2.37	2.59	2.35	2.53	2.78	2.74	2.22
1960	2.45	2.59	2.37	2.66	2.88	2.73	2.18
1961	2.49	2.79	2.42	2.57	2.91	2.82	2.22
1962	2.47	2.84	2.46	2.84	2.99	2.79	2.26
1963	2.69	2.83	2.53	2.85	3.02	2.89	2.32
1964	2.67	2.78	2.67	2.88	3.07	2.90	2.49
1965	2.53	2.69	2.63	2.81	2.96	2.83	2.42
1966	2.45	2.67	2.51	2.74	2.87	2.77	2.37
1967	2.36	2.62	2.44	2.63	2.84	2.64	2.28
1968	—	2.57	—	2.54g	2.77	2.58	2.09
1969	—	2.51	—	2.44g	2.62g	2.52	1.94
1970	—	2.30	—	2.38g	2.51g	—	1.94.

gUnofficial estimates calculated at the Office of Population Research from Office of Population Censuses and Surveys, The Registrar General's Quarterly Return for England and Wales, Quarter ended 30 June 1970.

males are born for every 1.0 females. To this 2.05 figure must be added a small amount of fertility to allow for the small proportion of women who currently fail to survive to the age of childbearing. Accordingly, a total fertility rate of 2.11 children per woman is required for replacement under low mortality conditions like those prevailing in the industrialized countries. For purposes of perspective, we shall arbitrarily define a total fertility rate of 2.25 as near-replacement fertility (this is a round figure about 5 percent above the 2.11 replacement figure).

Data on total fertility from 1945 to 1970 for 26 industrialized countries are summarized in Table 7-1.* First, we can see that near-replacement fertility has been by no means rare in industrialized countries since the end of World War II. Indeed, in many countries, total fertility rates of less than 2.25 have been quite common. (Near-replacement fertility was even more common before World War II, although space limitations have made it impossible to demonstrate this fact here.†)

Second, in many industrialized countries there is evidence of a marked decline in total fertility rates, especially since 1965. This is true of the two largest industrialized countries, the United States and the Soviet Union, as well as most of the others.

Third, the most marked fertility declines in the last decade have been those of Canada, the United States, Japan, Bulgaria, Czechoslovakia, Hungary, and Rumania (until 1967). These countries can be

* Except as indicated in the footnotes to Table 7-1, rates were taken from the following sources: United Nations, Department of Economic and Social Affairs, *Recent Trends in Fertility in Industrialized Countries* (New York, 1958), Table D; *United Nations Demographic Yearbook 1954* (New York, 1954), Table 21; *United Nations Demographic Yearbook 1965* (New York, 1966), Table 30; *United Nations Demographic Yearbook 1969* (New York, 1970), Table 31; *Population Index*, Vol. 35, no. 2 (April–June 1969), pp. 210–218; *New Zealand Official Yearbook 1971*, p. 94.

Gross reproduction-rate data were converted to estimates of total fertility rates using the sex-ratio estimates calculated in Pravin Vasaria, "Sex Ratio at Birth in Territories with a Relatively Complete Registration" (*Eugenics Quarterly*, Vol. 14 (1967), p. 132), as follows:

$$GRR_i \times (1.0 + Sex\ Ratio_i) = TFR_i$$

where i is a given country.

The exceptions to these procedures are as follows: The total fertility rates for the U.S.A., 1945–1968, were taken directly from official estimates in Vital Statistics of the United States, Vol. 1: *Natality* (Rockland, Md., 1970), Table 1-6. The total fertility rates given for Canada, 1945–1970, were taken directly from official estimates in *Statistics Canada, Vital Statistics 1970, Preliminary Annual Report* (Ottawa, May 1972). The total fertility rates given for Rumania, 1956–1970, are derived from Ghetau, V., "Consideratii asupra Indicelui de Reproducere a Populatiei" (*Revista de Statistica*, Vol. 12, 1971, p. 51).

† More extensive data are presented in Teitelbaum, 1972b.

classified into two types: those in which fertility control has been achieved largely by means of contraception and which experienced a sharp postwar increase in fertility from previously lower levels (Canada and the United States), and those where fertility control has been achieved largely by means of abortion and whose fertility has declined sharply from previously high levels (Japan, Bulgaria, Czechoslovakia, Hungary, and Rumania).

PATTERNS OF POSTWAR TOTAL FERTILITY

In the period from the end of World War II to the present, U.S. total fertility increased from 2.48 in 1945 to a peak of 3.77 in 1957 and then began to decline, at first gradually and later more precipitately, to a 1971 level estimated at 2.28 (and to a level for the first nine months of 1972 estimated at 2.04). The U.S. pattern is similar to that in three other countries—Canada, Australia, and New Zealand. It is instructive to compare this pattern with those followed by the other 22 industrialized countries discussed here.

Most of Western and Northern Europe, plus Australia, followed another pattern. This is characterized by a sharp but temporary (less than four years) "baby boom" after the end of World War II, followed by a gradual decline, a gradual increase, and another gradual decline. Four of the countries following this pattern (England and Wales, Sweden, Austria, and West Germany) experienced substantial periods of near-replacement fertility, and two (Austria and West Germany) dropped below replacement for about four years. In comparison with the Western and Northern European pattern, U.S. fertility was substantially higher for nearly 15 years of the postwar period, but has now declined to a level close to the median of these countries.

Finally, the remaining countries, comprising Eastern Europe and Japan, are characterized by more erratic fertility patterns. Even though all nine of these countries showed total fertility rates substantially above replacement in the immediate postwar period (or, in the cases of East Germany, Rumania, and the Soviet Union, when data became available in the 1950s), most have exhibited rather sharp declines over the quarter century since the war. Five (Bulgaria, Czechoslovakia, Hungary, Japan, and Rumania) dropped to or below replacement levels.

FUTURE IMPLICATIONS OF PAST
U.S. FERTILITY

Past fertility patterns have important implications for the future. Other things being equal, the higher the fertility of the recent past, the younger the age-distribution of the current population of women. The younger the age-distribution of women, the higher the crude birthrate and rate of natural increase for any given level of fertility. It follows, then, that the higher the fertility of the recent past, the higher will be the crude birthrate and rate of natural increase for any given level of fertility. In a sense, the current age-distribution contains within its structure a "momentum" factor determined by the recent past.

As has been noted, the U.S. and three other countries—Canada, Australia, and New Zealand—in contrast to most other industrialized countries, experienced substantial and relatively long-term fertility increases after World War II. This means that their current age-distributions contain greater momentum for population growth than do those of most industrialized countries. As an illustration of this point, consider the following: In order to achieve instant zero population growth (ZPG) from 1970 onward, the U.S. total fertility rate would have to decline 54 percent below the 1965–1970 level to a total fertility rate of 1.2. Similar, though even larger, declines would be required for the other three countries that experienced an extended postwar baby boom. In contrast, instant ZPG could be achieved in Belgium with a 20 percent decline in total fertility, in West Germany with a 16 percent decline, and in Austria with a 15 percent decline. (These data are presented in Table 7-2.)

Instant ZPG is not a likely eventuality in most countries, but the attainment of replacement-level fertility may be around the corner. For the same reason that instant ZPG would require fertility substantially below replacement in the U.S., fertility at replacement level would not mean instant ZPG. The momentum built into the age-distribution of a population means that if replacement fertility is achieved in a population that has previously been growing, the size of the population will continue to increase for some time to come. The proportion by which it will eventually increase under replacement conditions varies directly with its previous rate of growth. As may be seen in Table 7-2, replacement fertility in the United States would be followed by about 36 percent additional growth before a stationary population size would be achieved. This would mean a population of about 280

TABLE 7-2.   HYPOTHETICAL CALCULATIONS SHOWING THE FERTILITY
DECREASES REQUIRED TO MAKE POPULATION GROWTH CEASE
IN 1970-1975, AND THE POPULATION INCREASES IMPLIED BY
ACHIEVEMENT OF REPLACEMENT FERTILITY IN 1970-1975

Country	If population ceased to grow in 1970-1975		If replacement fertility were achieved in 1970-1975 and maintained to 2050	
	Hypothetical total fertility required in 1970-1975	Percent change from 1965-1970 total fertility	Hypothetical population size in 2050 (in millions)	Percent change from 1970 population size
Pattern I countries				
USA	1.2	−54%	279.2	+36%
Canada	1.0	−62	29.3	+43
Australia	1.1	−63	16.2	+36
New Zealand	N.A.*a*	N.A.*a*	N.A.*a*	N.A.*a*
Pattern II countries				
Switzerland	1.4	−42	7.2	+16
Austria	2.2	−15	8.5	+ 9
Italy	1.4	−44	66.9	+19
England and Wales	1.9	−27	55.8	+11
Scotland	1.8	−38	6.7	+20
France	1.7	−35	60.2	+17
Sweden	1.7	−26	8.6	+ 8
Denmark	1.5	−42	6.0	+19
Finland	1.2	−45	6.2	+26
Norway	1.5	−46	4.6	+19
West Germany	2.1	−16	67.1	+ 6
Belgium	2.0	−17	10.9	+12
Netherlands	1.2	−57	17.2	+32
Pattern III countries				
Bulgaria	1.3	−43	10.1	+19
Czechoslovakia	1.4	−33	17.8	+20
Hungary	1.6	−20	11.8	+11
Poland	1.1	−52	44.9	+33
Rumania	N.A.*a*	N.A.*a*	N.A.*a*	N.A.*a*
Yugolsavia	1.2	−54	28.2	+35
East Germany	2.4	+ 4	19.4	+ 5
USSR	1.3	−48	326.9	+26
Japan	0.8	−62	138.1	+30

Sources: Tomas Frejka, "Demographic Paths to a Stationary Population." In Demographic and
Social Aspects of Population Growth, Charles F. Westoff & Robert Parke, Jr., eds. Research Reports of
the Commission on Population Growth and the American Future, Vol. 1 (Washington: U.S.
Government Printing Office, 1972).

*a*N.A. = not available.

million by the middle of the next century. Table 7-2 also illustrates that the built-in population growth implied by the age structure of the United States is similar to those of Canada, Australia, and New Zealand, and markedly higher than those of most other industrialized countries.

LOW FERTILITY AND POSSIBLE REACTIONS

There is strong evidence that U.S. fertility has been declining sharply since 1965, and especially over the last year. The crude birthrate in the first nine months of 1972—about 15.5 per thousand—was the lowest in U.S. history. This is true even though the age-distribution is increasingly favorable to higher birthrates due to the maturation of the large number of baby boom babies from the 1950s. In such circumstances, the crude birthrate is distorted upward, meaning that the real decline in fertility is greater than the observed decline in the crude birthrate. As noted in Table 7-1, the best estimate of total fertility for the first nine months of 1972 is 2.04, which is fractionally below replacement level.

Demographers long ago learned to be wary of extrapolating current trends into the distant future. The current sharp declines in fertility may not continue. They may, for example, represent simply the postponement of eventual births due to economic conditions. The paradox of a situation where fertility behavior is under individual, voluntary control is that it is less predictable than when it is under the control of purely biological processes. We must therefore beware of *predicting* that U.S. fertility will drop below replacement level for a sustained period. At the same time, such a phenomenon is a real possibility for the first time since the 1930s. It might therefore be helpful to examine the reactions in countries that have already experienced such a situation. In the past, near-replacement or below-replacement fertility has often been perceived as a threat to the national well-being, in terms of both political power and economic prosperity. The pronatalist policies adopted by many European governments before World War II are well-known examples of such reactions. Recently, the Second European Population Conference reported renewed concern over near-replacement fertility and called for new pronatalist government measures (*Le Monde,* 1971; "Natalités Comparées," 1971). Between 1966 and 1971, three governments (Japan, Rumania, and Bulgaria) have discussed or have actually enacted measures to raise fertility because the rates were slightly below replacement. Brief case studies of Japan and Rumania are presented below.

Japan

After World War II, the issue of overpopulation was a serious one in Japan. Several population commissions were established, there was much comment in favor of birth control in the mass media, and the issue was discussed widely among the public. Some strong opposition to birth control was expressed at this time by Communist and Roman Catholic leaders. Nonetheless, the practice of fertility limitation, primarily via induced abortion, was practiced widely by Japanese women on a voluntary basis. The practice was facilitated by government action in 1948, when the Eugenics Protection Law was passed. This law provided support for family planning field workers; legalization of abortions for health reasons and, in 1949, for reasons of socioeconomic necessity; and legalization of sterilization for health reasons (Muramatsu, 1971).

Within 10 years after the end of World War II, Japanese total fertility declined by over 50 percent and in 1957 dropped below the replacement level. It has remained below replacement with the exception of the period between 1965 and 1967, during which birth patterns were sharply affected by the superstition of *hinoeuma* or the Year of Fire and Horse of the third sign of the zodiac.* Although the initial sharp decline in Japanese fertility was achieved by means of widespread abortion legalized under the Eugenic Protection Law, the 1950s saw a gradual shift away from abortion and toward contraception.

In the last several years a reaction against continued below-replacement fertility has developed in Japan. Pressures for increased fertility have arisen, particularly from industrial leaders, who have voiced concern over the developing shortage of young workers in the rapidly expanding economy. In August 1969, the Population Problems Inquiry Council of the Ministry of Health and Welfare issued an interim report urging measures to encourage a small increase in Japanese fertility in order to bring about a stationary population. The report was treated in a quite sensational manner by some elements of the mass media, which saw it as a warning of imminent national decline and urged a return to high fertility. Some publications interpreted the report to mean that the population of Japan was *already* declining. (It should be recalled that the mass media were among the primary supporters of fertility reduction in the postwar period.) The Japanese government is currently giving active consideration to a program of

* Although the total annual fertility during 1967 was above replacement level, that of 1966 was sharply depressed. The mean total fertility for the three years taken together was 1.98, very close to the mean for the period 1960–1964.

child allowances amounting to 3,000 yen ($8.30) per month to be provided to couples for their third child and each child thereafter. Although the government contends that this measure is entirely for purposes of child welfare, critics argue that it is in fact a pronatalist policy resulting from reaction to the below-replacement fertility of Japanese couples (Muramatsu, 1971).

Rumania

Total fertility data for Rumania are available only from 1955. In that year, total fertility was 3.07. A rapid and nearly linear rate of decline ensued, and fertility was below replacement by 1962. The most popular means of fertility control in Rumania was induced abortion, which was legalized in 1957. Abortions were attractive for a number of reasons: no approvals or bureaucratic procedures were required, secrecy was assured, the fee was low (less than $2), the danger was slight, and the only requirement was that the pregnancy be of less than 12 weeks duration. In contrast, little encouragement was given to contraceptive practice. Estimates by Mehlan and by the Rumanian Ministry of Health suggest nearly total dependence on abortion for fertility control by 1966 (David, 1970).

Official concern over the sharp decline in fertility, coupled with some evidence of growing laxity in medical procedures surrounding abortion, led the Rumanian government to an abrupt reversal of its policy on abortion. Decree No. 770, which went into effect November 1, 1966, limited abortion to cases involving risk to the mother's life, risk of congenital malformation, evidence of rape, pregnancy of women over 45 years of age, pregnancy of women supporting four or more living children, and a rigorously defined set of physical and psychological conditions (David, 1970). In addition to severely ristricting access to abortion, the Rumanian government instituted a battery of further pronatalist measures:

— Official importation of oral contraceptives and intrauterine devices was stopped. (Some supplies remained available at high prices on the Black Market, and condoms and creams continued to be produced domestically.)

— Taxes on unmarried and married but childless persons over 25 years of age were raised by 10 to 20 percent.

— Taxes on families with three or more children were reduced by 30 percent.

— Parents of large families could send their children to health resorts free of charge.

— Mothers of large families were promised early retirement from their jobs.

— Substantial birth premiums were offered following the birth of every child after the second.

— Divorces were made extremely difficult to obtain and the required fees raised to prohibitive levels.

— A series of official awards (including categories such as "Mother Heroine") were established to reward mothers of large families (West, 1969).

The fertility effects of these Rumanian policies were dramatic indeed. After the time lag expected for the gestation of pregnancies that previously would have been terminated by induced abortion, the crude birthrate rose steeply. For the year 1966 the crude birthrate was 14.3; for 1967 it was 27.4. The monthly crude birthrate reached a high of 39.9 in September 1967. The total number of live births in Rumania in 1967 was nearly twice that in 1966 (527,764 vs. 273,678). As may be seen in Table 7-1, total fertility rose from an estimated 1.90 in 1966 to 3.66 in 1967. The fertility increase following the 1966 measures undoubtedly represents the sharpest increase in the fertility of a large population in the history of the human species.

As with all dramatic demographic changes, the sharp increase in Rumanian fertility had important public and private effects and will continue to do so for many years. West quotes Rumanian newspaper accounts of three pregnant women sharing the same hospital bed and of doctors urging mothers to give birth at home during the peak fertility months of July, August, and September 1967 (West, 1969). The problem of inadequate facilities was compounded by the dependence of the Rumanian medical system upon female personnel, many of whom were forced to take maternity leave by the government's withdrawal of the primary means of fertility control.

As the children born in 1967 reach school age, an important problem will arise for educational administrators, who will have to accommodate an entering class twice as large as the one immediately preceding it. Similar, if attenuated, difficulties will arise as the 1967 birth cohort enters universities, the labor force, and so on.

The sharp increases in fertility, especially for older women and women with two or more children (Teitelbaum, 1972a), undoubtedly represent numerous cases of unwanted fertility, although the proportion will never be known with assurance. Although the increased government subsidies for later-born children may allow many of these unwanted children to escape the economic difficulties that might otherwise have resulted from their births, other psychological and social effects of the unwanted status may remain.

It is apparent that in the cases of Japan and Rumania, below-replacement fertility has been perceived as an undesirable state of affairs. The situations in the two countries differ in a number of respects. First, the Japanese fertility level had been below replacement for about 10 years before official concern became apparent, while the Rumanian legal change was implemented after less than six years of below-replacement fertility. Second, Japanese fertility is currently below replacement by means of both contraception and induced abortion, while Rumanian fertility in the period immediately preceding 1966 was controlled almost entirely by induced abortion. This difference has important policy implications; the means of fertility control can be far more easily withdrawn by government action when abortion under government auspices or license is the primary method than when contraception is in widespread use. Finally, the Japanese child allowance proposal cannot be compared with the draconian pronatalist measures implemented by the Rumanian government. The latter policies bear all the signs of overreaction, and the drastic changes in fertility are and will continue to cause considerable difficulties for the Rumanian people and their government.

The sensationalized response of some elements of the Japanese press and public to the sober report of the Population Problems Inquiry Council is of potential interest to Americans concerned with population policies in the U.S. If the current sharp decline in U.S. fertility continues to below-replacement levels, the U.S. government may wish eventually to discuss measures to increase this fertility to a level nearer replacement. In so doing, care will have to be exercised in order to avoid the type of public response aroused by the report of the Japanese Council. It is important that efforts be made now in the U.S. to encourage thoughtful consideration of the possibility of temporary below-replacement fertility and explicit recognition that this is not an unusual or threatening phenomenon.

SUMMARY AND IMPLICATIONS

Fertility at levels near or below replacement has been a common phenomenon in industrialized countries during the past half-century. Public and governmental response to low fertility has generally been negative, sometimes extremely so. In some cases, governments have implemented policies designed to sharply increase fertility, with consequent deleterious effects on individuals and on public services dealing with health and education.

Without any coercive antinatalist policies on the part of governments, sharp declines in fertility have occurred recently in many industrialized countries, including the U.S. The U.S. decline may continue to levels below replacement, and it is important to anticipate such a situation and encourage careful and restrained responses to it.

A number of policy implications derive from these considerations: (1) Population policies directed toward fertility should be carefully designed, with full awareness of the short- and long-term effects of excessively rapid changes in fertility rates. (2) The structure of such policies should be flexible and capable of affecting fertility rates both downward and upward in a gradual way. (3) The overall goal of such policies should be maintenance of fertility rates considered socially desirable, which in the U.S. is likely to mean levels near replacement over the long term. (4) Small intermediate-term (about 10 to 15 years) fluctuations below or above replacement are to be expected and should not be met with panic or sensationalized projection of future implications. (5) Recent evidence suggests that policies directed toward informed but free choice of fertility behavior may be sufficient to bring fertility to levels near or below replacement.

REFERENCES

DAVID, HENRY P. 1970. *Family Planning and Abortion in the Socialist Countries of Central and Eastern Europe.* New York: The Population Council, pp. 129–136.

Le Monde (English edition). September 11, 1971, p. 16.

MURAMATSU, MINORU. 1971. "Japan." In *Country Profiles.* New York: The Population Council, March 1971, pp. 6, 7.

"NATALITÉS COMPARÉES." 1971. In *Population et Societés,* Vol. 39 (1971), pp. 2–3.

TEITELBAUM, MICHAEL S. 1972a. "Fertility Effects of the Abolition of Legalized Abortion in Rumania." In *Population Studies,* Vol. 27 (November 1972), pp. 405–417.

———. 1972b. "International Experience with Fertility at or Near Replacement Level." In *Demographic and Social Aspects of Population Growth,* Charles F. Westoff & Robert Parke, Jr., eds. Research Reports of the Commission on Population Growth and the American Future, Vol. 1. Washington: U.S. Government Printing Office.

WEST, CHARLES V. 1969. "Rumania's Reluctant Mother Heroines of 1967." Unpublished typescript, pp. 6, 7–8.

NORMAN B. RYDER

8. The Future Growth
of the American Population

In 1972, the size of the population of the United States reached 209 million. Because of a massive fluctuation, in fertility, that size was grossly maldistributed by age, with few around age 35, many around age 15, and few around age 5. Over the past 18 months the birthrate has plunged to the unprecedentedly low figure of 15 per 1,000 per annum. These are the bits and pieces from which the demographer is asked to estimate our future population growth.

The present chapter begins with an illustrative projection, which will serve as the basis for more detailed comments. In the next section, we focus on the behavior that is at the core of the population future—the childbearing pattern—and speculate about the directions of change in reproductive intentions, and in the ability to fulfill those intentions. In conclusion, we discuss the most likely types of deviation from the base projection.

A caveat is appropriate at the beginning of this chapter: no demographer has ever succeeded in forecasting the future of any population. However, demographers today are much better informed

Norman B. Ryder is a professor of sociology and a faculty associate of the Office of Population Research at Princeton University. Most of his previous professional career was spent on the faculty of the University of Wisconsin. He has concentrated on methodological aspects of demography and studies of American fertility. He has just completed a term as president of the Population Association of America.

about the reasons for their failure, and their product is much more likely to be regarded with justifiable doubt. We call that progress.

AN ILLUSTRATIVE PROJECTION

To project a population into the future, we begin with the numbers of people, by age, currently in the population. Three questions must be answered in order to determine the future size of a population: How many people will die, age by age? How many births will occur, year by year? How many will be added to the population by international migration? The first question is the easiest to answer, because the likelihood of surviving from one age to the next has changed little in the recent past and is unlikely to change much in the foreseeable future. The answer to the third question obviously depends on our migration policy. The easy way out is to assume a continuation of the current net increase, which is about 400,000 per year. The bugaboo for the demographer is the question of future births. To indicate the difficulty: only 35 years ago about 2.4 million people were born each year; 10 years ago it was up to about 4.3 million; but in 1972, it appears likely that only about 3.2 million will be born.

What we do know is that we have large numbers of young people who are now entering their childbearing ages. This fact alone will mean large future birth crops, even if each couple aims at a small family size. Because of this circumstance, some demographers have predicted a second baby boom during the next decade and thus a large amount of future growth in population size. But developments in the theory of projection have indicated another factor that may counterbalance this factor—the time pattern of childbearing. If women were to bear their children at a somewhat later age than has previously been the case, their childbearing experience would be spread out and the amount of increase in births that we would otherwise expect would be dampened. There *is* evidence in this direction, although it is not clear how long and how far the tendency toward postponement will proceed.

At the behest of the Commission on Population Growth and the American Future, we recently produced a large set of projections and have selected one of those for exemplification (Ryder, 1973). The particular projection chosen is that which yielded the smallest ultimate population size compatible with a uniform number of future births each year, and based on a plausible set of ultimate reproductive values. The time series of growth data for this projection are shown in Table 8-1.

TABLE 8-1. BASE PROJECTION FOR THE UNITED STATES

Year	Population Size (in millions)	Decade Growth Rates (per thousand per year)				
		Increase	Birth	Migration	Death	Interval
1970	203.6	10.4	18.0	1.9	9.5	1970-80
1980	225.8	8.3	16.3	1.7	9.7	1980-90
1990	245.2	6.8	15.2	1.6	10.0	1990-2000
2000	262.5	5.5	14.3	1.5	10.3	2000-10
2010	277.3	4.0	13.6	1.4	11.0	2010-20
2020	288.7	2.4	13.2	1.3	12.1	2020-30
2030	295.7	0.7	13.0	1.3	13.6	2030-40
2040	297.7	0.0	12.9	1.3	14.2	2040-50
2050	297.8	0.0	12.9	1.3	14.2	2050-60
2060	297.9					

There are several noteworthy results. In the first place, population size increases by 46 percent (to its ultimate size of 298 million), even though there is a relatively brief lag before achievement of a replacement level of fertility. (The projection assumes that the cohort of 1960–1964, and every subsequent cohort, just reproduces itself.) The principal source of this growth is the large size of cohorts—currently 3.8 million—below the maximum age of childbearing. Our current population size of 203.6 million would be maintained (given a mean length of life in excess of 72) with a cohort size of only 2.8 million. Second, the growth is heavily concentrated in the early decades. Two-thirds of the absolute increase occurs within the first 30 years and growth essentially ceases by the end of the next 30 years. Finally, the earlier part of the transition in growth rate is caused primarily by a decline in the birthrate, whereas the later part of the transition is caused primarily by a rise in the death rate.

The rise in the death rate is caused by the transformation of the age distribution from one with a predominance of younger people to one with a predominance of older people. Figure 8-1 shows the 1970 age distribution (solid lines) and the ultimate age distribution that would go along with the projection in Table 8-1 (the outer dotted lines). The increase of approximately 100 million is essentially restricted to the adult population. The average age of the population rises from its current value of 32.3 to an ultimate 39.2.

The most striking contrast in Figure 8-1 is that between the irregularity of the current age distribution and the smoothness of the ul-

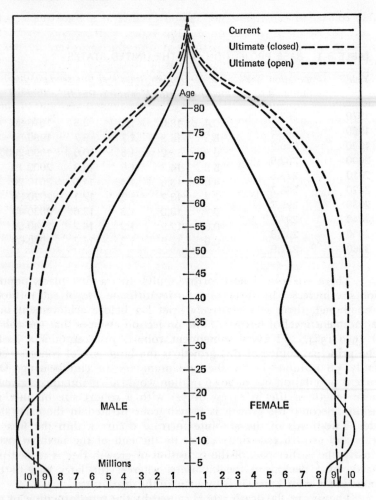

Figure 8-1. Distribution of the U.S. population by age and sex

timate pattern. Irregularity results primarily from changes in the number of births from year to year, which imply changes in the numbers at each succeeding age. Since so many sectors of the socioeconomic system have a clientele that is concentrated in particular ages (the school system, the labor market, the population on social security), they are affected not so much by change in population size as by change in cohort size. For example, each of these sectors is destined, in due course, to experience population decline as a consequence of the collapse of the birthrate during the 1960s. Furthermore, even if there were no change in the pattern of reproduction over the next generation, there would still be a somewhat muted echo of the cohort size fluctuations of the past 30 years in the size of cohorts during the next 30 years. This can be avoided if a rise in the average age of reproduction accompanies the decline of fertility, which was one of the assumptions underlying the projection we are using as an illustration here. Thus, although the distribution depicted is the ultimate stationery distribution, it is a very close approximation of the distribution we would obtain within two or three generations.

In order to show the effects of external migration on the shape of the stationary population, Figure 8-1 also indicates the age distribution of the ultimate population that is closed to migration (the inner broken lines). That age distribution is a carbon copy of the pattern of cohort survivorship age by age, with the youngest age group the largest. The stationary open age distribution, on the contrary, swells outward a little in the middle; its largest age group is 30–34. One index of the age distribution, frequently used because of its obvious economic import, is the dependency ratio: the ratio of those below age 15 and above age 65 to those between ages 15 and 65. In the current population, the value of this ratio is 0.62; in the closed stationary population it is 0.57; and in the open stationary population it is 0.56. Although most analysts tend to regard the prospect of an older population with disfavor, it does have the advantage of a lower dependency ratio. Moreover, the rise in the age of the population from an average of 32.3 to 39.2 can give a misleading impression about particular subdivisions of the population. For example, the average age of the population segment aged 25 to 54, which forms the core of the labor force, merely rises from the current 39.3 to an ultimate 39.9. Major changes are implicit in the transformation of the age distribution, especially the increase of the population over age 65 from 20 million to 49 million and the circumstance (presumably of considerable importance for career mobility) that the numbers of older persons in the labor force will be the same as the number of younger persons rather than, as now, much fewer. There may be no social question of comparable importance on which we have so little current wisdom as the consequences of transformation from a growing to a stationary age distribution.

SOME FUTURE POSSIBILITIES FOR FERTILITY

The projection we have just discussed is based on two major assumptions: (1) that the net reproduction rate will reach the replacement level soon, and (2) that the average age of reproduction will rise appreciably. In order to appraise the likelihood of these two assumptions, it is helpful to look at them in terms of what they would mean for the individuals involved. In a population that is open to external migration of the magnitude assumed above, the net reproduction rate designed to achieve replacement implies a mean of approximately two births per woman. Average fertility may be thought of as the product of the proportion of women fertile and the mean number of births per fertile woman. For example, an overall average of two births per woman need not imply that the two-child family is dominant. Such an average could be achieved if one-quarter remained infertile (whether or not they married), one-quarter had two children, and the remaining one-half had three children. A high proportion of infertile women would not be unprecedented in American vital statistics: only 77 percent of the cohort of 1909 eventually had any children.

Currently, mean fertility is less than 2.4. It has declined, over the past 10 to 15 years, from a modern peak of 3.3. Although the principal cause of this recent decline has been a reduction in the number of unwanted births, declining reproductive intentions have also played an important role. Since we have fertility rates specific for order of birth only through 1968, it is difficult to make a clear statement about the amount of recent change in the proportion fertile, but the direction is clearly downward. For example, by age 24 the proportion fertile for the cohort of 1935 was 71 percent, whereas the proportion fertile for the cohort of 1945 was 62 percent. Although that kind of change may have occurred as a consequence of a rise in the mean age at first birth, the evidence to date suggests that this is unlikely.

It is evident from the discussion in the first section of this chapter that the outcome of a projection is highly sensitive to changes in the average age of reproduction. Not surprisingly, the average age of reproduction varies directly with the average age at first birth and with the length of an average birth interval. Less obviously, it also varies directly with the extent of heterogeneity in the sizes of families. To use an extreme example, an average fertility of two can be achieved if every woman has two children or if half of the women have no children and the other half have four each. The mean age of reproduction would be greater in the latter case than the former. We conclude that, of the various distributions of completed fertility by which replacement can be achieved, there is an advantage in terms of smaller ultimate population size to those in which there is greater reproductive heterogeneity.

What current and prospective developments in the causal system underlying our demographic parameters are relevant to the plausibility of the base projection? The question can be divided into considerations affecting, first, the means toward reproductive ends and, second, the reproductive ends themselves. With respect to the former, we are in the midst of a veritable revolution in fertility regulation (see Chapter 3). There has been a fundamental transformation of the practice of contraception within a very short time. This change is not so much the greater use of contraception—since that has been close to a maximum for some time—but rather the use of more effective methods, particularly the oral contraceptive and the intrauterine device, and the earlier initiation of effective contraceptive methods. Three important consequences for population projections derive from this revolution and they are already evident in current data: reduction of the amount of unintended fertility; rise in the age at first birth; and lengthening of the interval between births.

The revolution in fertility regulation also encompasses sterilization and abortion. Among older women in the reproductive ages, sterilization (of themselves or their husbands) is now the principal means for terminating exposure to the risk of unintended conceptions. Legalized abortion is a quite recent development and of limited availability, but this will change rapidly as a result of the recent Supreme Court decision. It already appears to be a significant influence on the birthrate. Its principal demographic importance probably derives from its potential role in raising the age at first birth and decreasing the probability of failure for the voluntarily infertile. Given the fundamental questions about control over life and sexual behavior that are raised by abortion, it is not surprising that it has provoked ideological struggle in the courts, the legislatures, and the churches. Nevertheless, in long-run perspective, the most likely prospect would seem to be increasing adoption of this procedure—until the time when contraception and sterilization make it unnecessary.

The revolution in fertility regulation means that individuals and couples are in a much better position to fulfill their reproductive intentions, whatever they may be. Current data from the 1970 National Fertility Study, together with inferences from contemporary vital statistics, support the thesis that the improvement in the quality of fertility regulation is the principal source of the decline of fertility between 1960 and 1970 (see Chapter 6). With due recognition for the difficulties of interpretation of statistics on reproductive intentions, the same sources suggest that if the current size of intended family were achieved it would yield a level of fertility very close to replacement.

The task of making reasonable inferences about future reproductive intentions for the purpose of population projection is exceedingly hazardous, because both our theoretical framework and our data base are quite inadequate. With that warning as a preface, we suggest that the most important current trend concerns the status of women. It is our judgment that women are going to move toward much more equal access to education and employment than heretofore and that this will substantially increase the attractiveness of alternatives to motherhood. It may well be that fertility sufficient for replacement was achieved in the past only by a combination of a system of sex control that made parenthood the price males and females had to pay for sexual enjoyment and a system of labor control that blocked women from positions of prestige, power, and profit. If freer choices for women are a reality in the future, the principal demographic consequences would seem to be an increase in the proportion voluntarily infertile and a rise in the average age at first birth.

Perhaps the principal development that leads analysts to expect higher rather than lower fertility in the future is the likelihood that productivity will continue to increase over the long run, and, with it, real income per capita. This may be so, but there are various qualifications that raise doubts:

1. One condition for continually rising productivity is a rising level of education. That activity is competitive with the parental role —particularly with early parenthood.

2. There is a strong inverse correlation between cohort size and cohort reproduction, reflecting the difficulties, particularly on entry into the labor force, of competition with a large number of contemporaries. Since the size of the cohort entering the labor force will continue to rise for at least another decade, there is a plausible case, in the short run, for a projection in which the time pattern of reproduction moves upward.

3. The consequences of a rise in per capita income depend on the distribution of the increase among the income classes. In the past, a substantial part of our citizenry have not participated fully in the general societal advance. Should we choose to remedy this grievance by extending a decent minimum level of income and health to all, it is a moot question whether the fertility of those now below that minimum would rise or fall. The higher current fertility of the disadvantaged probably reflects mainly their sense of futility about personal improvement.

4. Should income growth continue to accrue to the middle- and upper-income groups as much as or more than to the poor, the question is whether they will use some of the additional income to finance additional children. Empirical evidence, as distinct from logical persuasiveness, is at least ambiguous on the subject.

5. Even the thesis that income will rise—in a sense that it is relevant to reproductive intentions—can be questioned, at least for the next generation or two. In the first place, the ecology debate has made us aware that the rise in our gross national product has concealed the accumulation of a large environmental debt and that we must now start paying for many goods that we regarded as free. Second, the greater growth in per capita income of the rich than of the poor nations is unsettling in the short run and probably intolerable in the long run. Whether our response to this challenge takes the form of expenditures on either arms or development capital—and it will probably be both—the immediate prospect is that the problems of the impoverished majority of mankind will cost dearly.

The many judgments in this section have less than high credibility. Even at their best—that is, when they sound plausible—they indicate direction rather than extent of change. Regrettably, such are the kinds of judgments that dominate the solution of the projection problem.

CONCLUSION

The final task is to consider the most likely ways in which the base projection will depart from reality. The first potential problem is the assumption that replacement fertility will be achieved soon and maintained thereafter. There is no direct and simple link between a macro-demographic average, like the net reproduction rate, and the fertility intentions of individuals and their fulfillment; no thermostat modifies intentions down and efficacy up whenever the net reproduction rate exceeds replacement. There are macro-demographic consequences of reproductive surpluses and deficits, and these may impinge on fertility, but the response is likely to lag considerably behind the stimulus and is unlikely to be so finely calibrated as to restore equilibrium. A growth rate of one-half of 1 percent per year, positive or negative, even if maintained for only a generation, would produce a change of population size of approximately 14 percent.

Even if fertility in the long run averaged out at the replacement level, the vital history of the past 50 years emphasizes the strong probability of short-run upward and downward movements in the number of births per year, and thus in the sizes of cohorts at successively higher ages. Such fluctuations are unlikely to cease. With the approach of something like accurate fertility regulation, they may even become sharper. That is to say, if the same kinds of stimulus that provoked reproductive responses in the past occur in the future, the responses will probably be more immediate and larger in magnitude. The collapse of the birthrate since the early 1960s suggests that kind of future.

The projection treated the possibility of substantial improvement in survivorship with cavalier neglect. To gauge the magnitude of this effect, we posited a decline of 20 percent in all of the age-specific probabilities of death, from the levels assumed in the projection. There are two consequences, one minor and the other moderate. The first concerns a rise in the proportion surviving to childbearing age (the survivorship component of the net reproduction rate). That effect is so small that it could be counterbalanced by a decline in fertility of 0.6 percent. The second consequence would be an increase of 4.6 percent in the mean length of life, and thus an increase in the ultimate population size (were the assumed mortality decline to take place) from 298 to 312 million. The increase in length of life is proportionately much smaller than the decrease in mortality because, in a low-mortality population like ours, those who are spared death are mostly in ages at which the additional years of life to be expected are in any event few.

The base projection followed the migration assumption used in the official projections (4 million per decade). This is a high average. Our current foreign-born population represents the outcome of something closer to 2.5 million per decade. The implication of the base projection, distinguishing the native-born from the foreign-born, is that the former is scheduled to increase by some 40 percent, but the latter by some 100 percent. It seems not unlikely that as fertility approaches replacement and as population growth approaches zero the migratory flow will be reduced below its current level.

Projections are obviously useful for future planning, if the analyst is lucky enough to come close to the mark. They are also useful when they fail, because the reasons for their failure can be used to reduce our stock of ignorance. The reproductive behavior at the root of any projection is now experiencing rapid and comprehensive transformation. In the circumstances, we should invest heavily in fertility research in order to make projections like the present one obsolete. The primary purpose of this chapter has been not so much to convince the reader of the likelihood of the projection presented as to advertise the kinds of input that make more or less difference to the outcome, and thus the points at which criticism can be most telling. The proper stance for the maker of a population projection is humility. The proper stance for the user is skepticism.

REFERENCE

RYDER, N. B. 1973. "A Demographic Optimum Projection for the U.S. Population." In *Demographic and Social Aspects of Population Growth*, Charles F. Westoff & Robert Parke, Jr., eds. Research Reports of the Commission on Population Growth and the American Future, Vol. 1. Washington: U.S. Government Printing Office, pp. 605–22.

STEPHEN ENKE

9. The Impact of Population Growth on the National Economy

INTRODUCTION

Most people feel that gross national product (GNP) is related to population growth in the United States—but they disagree as to whether a faster or slower population growth rate improves living standards. Because population growth has been associated with economic growth in U.S. history, some fear that zero population growth (ZPG) would mean zero economic growth also. Many businessmen appear to have an almost atavistic belief that an increasing population is somehow "good for business." Recent reductions in U.S. fertility rates, together with increasing fears that a growing population and GNP damage the environment, have increased popular interest in the GNP-to-population relation (Kuznets, 1967; Ohlin, 1967). However, despite this interest, no certain method of establishing this relationship yet exists.

THE HISTORICAL ASSOCIATION

Throughout the history of the United States, and especially during the period between the Civil War and World War I, population

Dr. Stephen Enke is Consulting Economist at TEMPO, in Washington, D.C. He has served on the staffs of UCLA, RAND, Yale, Duke, IDA, and the Secretary of Defense. In 1969 he directed a presidential review of Selective Service.

growth and economic growth were closely and clearly associated. This past association has led many to believe that a cessation of population growth would somehow result in a braking of economic growth, so that economic welfare, as reflected in per capita income, would in the future grow slowly, if at all. However, association is not causation, and there are no reasons for believing that ZPG a half century from now would end U.S. economic growth.

The following are some of the reasons why the past may not be a reliable guide to the future in this connection.

First, the influence of technology, meaning the introduction of new methods of production and distribution in both industry and agriculture, was very great. Approximately two-thirds of the improvement in real income per capita during the period from 1865 to 1914 appears to be attributable to such advances in the "state of the arts." The productivity of capital and labor inputs, although difficult to measure, is probably increasing at about 2.5 percent annually. There is no reason to suppose that new inventions and methods will not continue to be introduced in the future. Accordingly, even if there were no increase in the use of capital per worker, one could expect real income per head to be roughly 2.1 times greater in 30 years and 3.4 times greater in 50 years.

Second, during this interwar period, capital was flowing into the U.S. from Europe, creating new jobs and expanding the nation's output. This relatively large capital inflow was not permanent. Since World War I, public and private investment capital have been flowing *from* the United States. This is likely to continue for the rest of the century. The result is to lessen future growth in gross *domestic* product (made within the U.S.), but not in GNP, of course (because overseas investments typically earn a profit or interest return).

Third, the effect of population growth on land availability was only moderate until the end of the last century. As the Atlantic States filled, in terms of the ratio of people to profitably usable land, their population overflowed into the Middle West and across the Great Plains to the Far West. The possibility of "taking up" land further west and earning a fair livelihood, given the standards of the times, maintained workers' wages and encouraged further internal migration.

Fourth, a small but significant percentage of the annual population increase came from immigration. The addition of adult immigrants (especially if they are trained in useful skills) rather than native infants is the economically preferable way of increasing population. Although some immigrants brought very young children and others sent financial remittances overseas, their overall impact on the nation's economy in the period between the Civil War and World War I was extremely favorable. On the whole, these new citizens provided an economically beneficial form of population increase that will never occur again on the same relative scale.

Fifth, and most decisively, statistical associations—even over long time periods—do not necessarily indicate any causal interaction. During most of the nation's history, almost everything has been increasing, including the number of alcoholics and gravestones, yet no one assumes that these have been a cause of economic growth.

VIEWS OF BUSINESSMEN

A majority of businessmen have an almost instinctive belief that growth of any kind is "good for business." This view is invalid if it means that faster is always better than slower when it comes to population growth. But it is not difficult to understand why this common opinion is often so vigorously upheld.

More population means more customers, which means more sales and gross income, which for a while at least means more profits. However, after a while, extra sales require a greater investment in plant and equipment to expand capacity, so that even though absolute profits may increase, the profit return per unit of capital may not long remain abnormally high. Moreover, if an area becomes more populated with customers, it may very well become more populated with rival firms. This is especially true in service industries, such as motels, restaurants, and all retail outlets.

Finally, when considering whether a slow or rapid increase in U.S. population over the next half century might be good or bad for business, it needs to be recognized that a faster population growth will almost certainly result in each person typically having less real income to spend. The businessman who has experienced profits because he was established in a rapidly expanding area such as California, Texas, or Florida does not assume that more local population means more *poorer* customers. However, when considering different population growth rates for the whole U.S., the choice is probably between many more people with some extra real income to spend or fewer extra people with much more real income to spend. (There were more people in the U.S. in 1933 than 1929, but they spent less, and business was depressed.) What businessmen want, like everyone else, is a future that provides a high real output, and hence a high real income per person.

EFFECTS OF POPULATION GROWTH
ON INDUSTRIES

If a rapid rate of population growth means a slower increase in real per capita output and income—for the reasons advanced in the next section—it follows that some industries will suffer comparatively more than others from rapid population growth.

The sales of some industries are income elastic; that is, as family incomes rise by x percent, these industries sell more than proportionately extra. Most service industries are in this category. So are most durable consumer goods industries (such as appliances, automobiles, residential construction). The producers of such goods should severally favor slower rates of population growth.

Other industries have sales that are income inelastic; if real income per family rises on an average by x percent, they will sell less than x percent extra to a typical family. Potato growers and linoleum manufacturers should accordingly not favor a slow population growth with a fast increase in real per capita income.

Superficially, it would seem that some industries must profit from a faster population growth, because the number of items they sell depends upon the number of customers. Examples might be shoe manufacturers and pediatricians. Certainly, the more people, the more feet to shoe; but men and women buy more or fewer shoes, of better or poorer quality, depending on their individual incomes. Admittedly, the more babies, the greater the *need* for pediatricians; however, because a larger fraction of families are unable to *afford* pediatric services, the practices of pediatricians may prove more profitable if there are fewer babies and more families with higher incomes.

Moreover, even if population growth were to slow, most industries have a long time to adjust. Morticians typically know how many customers they will have during the next 70 years or so—their customers during this period are already born and their number published by the census. Manufacturers of appliances, whose sales depend significantly on new family formations, can similarly predict the number of first marriages for the next 25 years or so. Perhaps the most vulnerable industry is diaper manufacturing, for a decline in fertility has an almost immediate effect on its sales. Yet it is estimated that even if all families had no more than two children each, future annual births would never fall below 1971 births (Frejka, 1968). Reduced fertility should not reduce future profits.

ECONOMIES OF SCALE

Another common view is that extra population within a region provides important economies of scale: expensive undertakings can be shared among many and thus become economical. Adam Smith was one of the first to observe that labor specialization depends on the size of the market. And it has long been part of the American tradition, stemming from pioneer days near the frontier, that extra population is economically desirable because it permits the construction of bridges, railroads, and other infrastructure, at costs per user that can be justified.

Some of today's metropolitan concentrations of population may have an analogous rationale. Part of the cohesion of these concentrations is explained by our highly varied product and service economy. Many luxury goods can only be found in really large cities. Moreover many of the people who have to live in places like New York, because of the financial and other contacts that they offer, can afford to pay the higher living costs.

In our complex and varied economy, some goods and services can be provided economically to a small market, but others cannot. Few parts of the U.S., except for Alaska and some of the Great Plains States, today need extra population to provide infrastructure. Highly specialized services, however, such as opera, do require large population concentrations. Nevertheless, for the production of commonly used goods and services, the U.S. market is already large enough. There can be few if any goods or services that are not available in the U.S. because it provides too small and poor a market.

THEORETICAL RELATION BETWEEN
POPULATION AND ECONOMIC GROWTH

Some Conceptual Relations

Economists can perhaps shed some light on the probable relationship between growth in population and GNP. Some computer simulations of future growth patterns include some quite complex interactions. Described below is one of the simplest ways of explaining why a slowing population can be expected to result in higher per capita incomes than would a continuing high population growth rate.

GNP, or national income, is generally considered to be a function of labor force, total capital stock, and technology (or "state of the art"). A growing population means a growing labor force. However, the productivity of this labor force, for a rather constant rate of employment, depends very much upon the capital-to-worker ratio.

The amount that will be saved from a given-sized GNP can be expected to be greater the smaller the population that might consume it. Declining age-specific fertility rates have the effect of aging the population because there are relatively fewer children as a result. The ratio of nonproducing dependents, and especially the ratio of child dependents per adult gainfully employed, hence also declines. Families begin to save a larger fraction of their incomes. These savings become investments that increase the nation's capital stock. Annual increments in capital stock are likely to vary positively with GNP and negatively with population.

The Commission on Population Growth and the American Future, based on Bureau of Census projections, estimated that by 2000 the dependency ratio would be 62, if all families had two children. That is, for every 100 persons of age 18 through 64, there would be 62 people either under 18 or over 64. The three-child-per-family projection puts this same dependency ratio at 80, which means 18 more dependents per 100 work-age adults and less saving from a given GNP.

Accordingly, if the choice is between a rapid or slow increase in population, the former will generate a larger labor force, which in turn will generate increments in GNP. A more slowly increasing population and labor force would produce a more slowly increasing GNP, if other things were equal. But they are not equal. Depending on savings rates, the more slowly growing labor force may find itself equipped with so much more equipment (capital) that in the aggregate it produces almost the same absolute GNP. Almost the same GNP increase, associated with a much smaller population increase, means more output and income per person when measured in constant prices.

Moreover, regardless of labor force size and capital stock size, advancing technology is increasing the output per unit of employed labor and capital. This annual productivity improvement is probably independent of population growth rates. Of course, productivity may increase a little more rapidly if there is a higher rate of investment per worker, because new technologies are very largely capital-embodied in new labor-saving equipment. Nevertheless, improvements in productivity are here considered as a function of time. Hence, the more slowly some population level such as 300 million is approached, the more readily can capital increments outpace labor force increments.

In addition, more years intervene during which improved technology can increase productivity at a compounded rate (Enke, 1971).

A Numerical Example

An example of the effects of population growth on GNP per capita for the United States are afforded by some alternative projections (TEMPO, 1970).

Two fertility projections are assumed. In the high-fertility case, it is assumed that there are no reductions in age-specific fertility rates. In the low-fertility case, it is assumed that birthrates decline sufficiently to attain a replacement level by year 2000. With high fertility, a population of 308 million is attained by 2000. With low fertility a population of 279 million is attained by 2000.

The economic results of these two alternative demographic projections were calculated. It was assumed that productivity increased 2.0 percent a year, compounded. An x percent increase in employed labor force was assumed to give a 0.6 x percent increase in GNP, while a y percent increase in capital stock was assumed to increase GNP by 0.35 y percent. Savings were set at 7 percent of GNP, an assumption that probably overstates the GNP with high population and understates it with low population.

It was also supposed that the American people continue to exploit their rising living standards by working less. The average number of days worked was presumed to decrease by 0.5 percent a year during the 60 years. (Thus a fully employed person would work 250 days a year in 1970, but only 175 days a year in 2030.)

Table 9-1 contrasts the GNP per capita that results from these

TABLE 9-1. PROJECTIONS OF POPULATION AND GNP FOR THE UNITED STATES (WITH INCREASING LEISURE)

Year	High Fertility[a]			Low Fertility[b]		
	Population (in millions)	GNP (in billions)	GNP Per Capita	Population (in millions)	GNP (in billions)	GNP Per Capita
1980	233	$1,172	$ 5,027	231	$1,172	$ 5,087
1990	268	1,651	6,158	256	1,649	6,433
2000	308	2,378	7,730	279	2,340	8,384
2010	356	3,428	9,636	301	3,258	10,830
2020	411	4,888	11,899	320	4,399	13,740
2030	471	7,277	15,445	333	6,014	18,056

[a]No decline in fertility rates.

[b]Fertility declines steadily until a net reproduction rate of unity is attained in 2000.

alternative population growths. By 2030 absolute GNP is $7,277 billion with high fertility and $6,014 billion with low fertility, because of the more than proportionately larger labor force in the former case. However, in terms of GNP per head, high fertility gives $15,445 a year as against $18,056 per head with low fertility. Per capita income with slower population growth is thus 1.16 times, or about $2,600 a year, greater by 2030. (These values are in constant 1970 prices.)

Incidence on Employees, Capitalists, and Owners of Land

Although a slower population growth apparently provides a higher future standard of living on an *average*, people earn their livelihoods in various ways, and so certain classes of people are benefited more than others. Some, for example, earn their incomes entirely from salaries and wages. Others earn their incomes largely from property, whether capital or land (including natural resources and real property).

As already seen, one outcome of a slower population growth is a larger capital stock relative to the number of full-time worker equivalents. As a result, the value of labor increases relative to that of capital. For example, by 2020, it is estimated that a full-time average employee would have annual earnings of $31,600 with low fertility and $30,400 with high fertility. The return on capital, however, is estimated at 15.5 percent with high fertility and 14.4 percent with low fertility. (This follows from the estimate that the capital-per-worker ratio is $84,100 with high and $93,700 with low fertility.)

It does not necessarily follow, however, that capitalists suffer from slower population growth. In this case, the stock of capital is almost what it would be with high fertility. Also, with low fertility there may be fewer capitalists as well as fewer people. In this event, the income from capital per capitalist is about 16 percent greater with low rather than high fertility.

It might seem that a smaller future population must at least hurt owners of land financially. The annual rent value of individual pieces of land will typically be lower if the population is 333 million instead of 471 million in 2030. However, the stock of land is the same, and with fewer people there are probably fewer owners of land. If the share of GNP that is paid for the use of land remains constant, landowners are better off with slower population growth. Moreover, to be realistic, the value of a particular piece of land almost 60 years from now is going to depend far more on other factors than national population growth: for example, the use to which it is put, the quality of the immediately surrounding area, and local population distribution.

In any event, according to modern economic welfare, it does not matter if some persons might be disadvantaged by a situation that benefits the economy on an average. It is then possible for those who are advantaged to compensate fully those that are disadvantaged and still remain better off themselves. Hence, if one accepts the above projections, the overall gains from a slower rate of population growth could in theory be redistributed so that everybody would be better or no worse off economically than they would be with a more rapid increase in population.

UNEMPLOYMENT AND LEISURE

It is sometimes argued that a slower population growth may result in higher rates of unemployment among the labor force. Lower fertility rates could put more women in the labor force. An aging population, with proportionately more people over 60, may seem to imply too many men and women who are too old to work.

Slower population growth rates could result in lower unemployment rates, however. Much of today's unemployment is among those entering the job market for the first time. Lower fertility rates will eventually reduce the percentage of population between 20 and 25 years, perhaps giving them something of a scarcity value for certain kinds of jobs. More of those above age 60 could be working if more employers would provide more part-time jobs.

The most striking feature of all these demographic-economic projections is that a per capita income five times that of today can be expected within 50 years—even with a 30 percent reduction in work per year. Material incentives to work eight hours a day for 250 days a year will be much reduced. Gainfully employed adults will increasingly wish to "buy back their time," working perhaps three ten-hour days a week in industry, permitting plants to operate a more intensive six-day week on two shifts. As people earn more per hour in real terms, they can afford more leisure. But hours at leisure ordinarily occasion more dollars worth of consumption per hour than do hours at work. And so a slowly changing leisure-to-earnings balance can be expected in the future, with ever more total leisure per person and ever more consumption resulting from leisure-type activities.

POPULATION AND POLLUTION

One of the commonly advanced arguments in favor of slowing population growth is that it would reduce the increase in pollution that can otherwise be expected. This argument seems implicitly to hold that people as people create pollution. However, aside from obvious human wastes, mere population size will probably do less to pollute the environment than will geograpic concentrations of population and higher levels of GNP.

The present population of the United States would pollute the environment less intolerably if it were uniformly distributed geographically. The same number of cars might be exhausting the same volume of fumes, the same number of beer cans might be discarded, but a given level of annoyance might be attainable at a smaller total prevention and clean-up cost. Part of today's smog nuisance and garbage disposal costs are attributable to increasing geographic concentrations of population.

More important still as a contributor to pollution is the absolute level of GNP. More GNP means more industrial fumes, more scrap, and more noise, among other things. Doubling the GNP could double the extent of pollution in these forms, even though the population remained almost constant. Recycling waste and/or requiring disposable containers are only partial remedies. In most cases they involve economic costs and thus augment GNP (as measured today).

It is therefore significant that a reduction in fertility, which slows population growth, can in turn result in a smaller GNP. Also, the smaller the national population at any future date, the smaller are likely to be the metropolitan concentrations of population, and it is these concentrations that seem to increase almost exponentially the costs of dealing with pollution. Hence, through reduced fertility, a typical citizen should suffer less from pollution, while enjoying a higher material standard of living.

A slower rate of population growth accordingly serves the counter-pollution cause in several ways, not primarily because there will be a smaller total population living within the United States at any given future date, but because there may well be a smaller than otherwise GNP.

In considering projections over half a century, however, the use of GNP as some measure of well-being is seen to have serious limitations. On one side, as population and GNP increase, an ever-larger fraction of the activities that are included in this measure are things like garbage removal, anti-smog devices, and commuter travel, none of which are pleasurable and many of which would otherwise not be necessary. Conversely, as GNP per capita increases severalfold, more people can enjoy increased consumption, along with an increased voluntary leisure that is not counted into GNP.

CONCLUSIONS

A number of generalizations can be made about the interactions of population growth and economic advance, that are probably as applicable to other nations as they are to the U.S.

The economic incidence of a given population growth rate depends somewhat upon whether it is associated with high birth and death rates or with low birth and death rates. A country with crude birth and death rates of 25 and 15 respectively per 1,000 population a year is likely to have a higher standard of living than one with birth and death rates of 35 and 25 respectively—even though both are growing at the same percentage rate. In the former low-rate case, there will be a smaller proportion of children who are too young to produce, but certainly old enough to consume. There is less waste of life at most ages. There are also fewer unwanted births.

Further, a nation may maintain a constant rate of natural increase, but be experiencing gradually lower crude birth and death rates. The very fact that these rates are declining provides certain economic advantages. During this decline there can be increased savings, because there are fewer children than there would otherwise be, but the subsequent loss in labor is not experienced for 20 years or so. Meanwhile, increased saving means more capital and output per worker, and there are more workers relative to the total population. The result is more output per worker and an even higher value output per head of population.

With regard to the U.S., no convincing argument has been made that it needs more people. As for the U.S. rate of population growth, the slower this can be, the more opportunity there is for annual savings to increase the capital-to-worker ratio, and the more time there is for improvements in technology to increase productivity before a certain population size is attained. So far as U.S. fertility is concerned, a period of declining fertility brings numerous advantages as indicated, and when the transition is completed it leaves a population with a higher proportion of employable adults.

Economics is far from being an exact science. It is probably significant, however, that plausible arguments in favor of *faster* population growth hardly seem to exist. The weight of argument is all in favor of an earlier rather than a later attainment of ZPG.

REFERENCES

ENKE, STEPHEN. 1971. "Economic Consequences of Rapid Population Growth." In *Economic Journal*, Vol. 81, no. 324 (December 1971), p. 800–811.

FREJKA, T. 1968. "Reflections on the Demographic Conditions Needed to Establish a U.S. Stationary Population Growth." In *Population Studies*, Vol. 22 (November 1968), pp. 379–397.

KUZNETS, S. 1967. "Population and Economic Growth." In *Proceedings of the American Philosophical Society*, Vol. 3 (1967), pp. 170–193.

OHLIN, G. 1967. *Population Control and Economic Development.* Paris: Organization for Economic Cooperation and Development.

TEMPO. 1970. "Zero U.S. Population Growth—When, How, and Why." Washington: General Electric's Center for Advanced Studies.

10. The Impact of Population Growth on Resources and the Environment

If the population of the United States continues growing at recently experienced rates, it will be some 50 percent larger within another half century. At that point, the gross national product, assuming only a steady 4 percent growth rate, could be as much as seven times its current size. However, these magnitudes will never be reached if the current growth rate of pages devoted to the resource-environment-population issue continues, for it will take no more than 10 to 15 years before we drown in paper.

The recent explosion of concern about our resource and environmental base represents a highly welcome goad to action. But most writers on the subject disagree with each other in practically every way possible—on the nature and severity of the problem, on its causes and remedies, and on how much time we have to mend our ways. These disagreements have led to actions that are less directed than might otherwise have been the case. In the hope—perhaps the vain hope—of remedying this situation, as well as to sort out for ourselves the

Ronald Ridker is an economist with Resources for the Future, Inc., in Washington, D.C. He was formerly an economic advisor to the AID mission on population programs in India and a professor of economics at Washington University in St. Louis.

The author is especially grateful to his wife, Carol Ridker, for her help in editing this paper.

complex issues involved, Resources for the Future recently added two contributions to the torrent of paper on the subject. The first is a book (Brubaker, 1972) that attempts to separate the important from the unimportant and the known from the unknown and that we hope will provide the reader with a proper perspective and sense of proportion. The second is a study undertaken for the Commission on Population Growth and the American Future (Ridker, 1972), which takes a quantitative look at a number of problems raised in the Brubaker book and asks what the situation with respect to these problems might be in the future under alternative assumptions about population growth, economic growth, and the implementation of various environmental policies.

In this chapter it is not possible to do justice to the major conclusions of either of these studies. Instead, general features of the report to the Population Commission, and their policy implications, will be discussed. First, an outline of the approach will be reviewed; then three of the principal findings will be examined; and, finally, a few comments about other approaches and implications for policy will be added.

THE APPROACH

Four factors characterize the approach taken in the study for the Population Commission. First, we concerned ourselves with a specific, selected group of resources, pollutants, and environmental pressures associated with population and economic growth in the United States during the next quarter to half century. This is the shortest time period within which to observe significant effects of a change in the population growth rate, but the longest period within which we can have any modicum of confidence in our ability to say something useful about the future. Although gross estimates of demand and supply for resources in the rest of the world were used (largely to make sure that U.S. raw material import needs could be met at reasonable prices), they were not studied in detail. An attempt was made to include representative resources and environmental threats, but because of data problems—particularly in the environmental field—we were not completely successful. Thus, had this study focused on some other country (particularly a poor country), on a longer time period, or on some other environmental threats, our conclusions might have been quite different. We would like to have been more general, but we found that we could not do so and maintain any reasonable degree of confidence in our conclusions.

Second, instead of attempting to forecast, we specified a number of hypothetical circumstances—scenarios—specifically chosen for their policy relevance. Four were chosen: one represents a low rate of growth in both population and the economy, another represents a high rate of growth in both these factors, and the remaining two are the intermediate cases. If we found that the supply of resources appear to be adequate during the next 50 years even when the high-population/ high-economic growth case is assumed, or that these are inadequate even when the low-population/low-economic growth case is assumed, we have conclusions with strong policy implications despite our inability to forecast just what will happen. Cases that permitted us to draw conclusions of this kind were emphasized. At best, therefore, our conclusions should be viewed as highly conditional projections, based on assumptions that were chosen for their policy relevance and not necessarily because we believe they are the most likely to occur in practice.

Third, so far as assumptions with respect to tastes, technology, and institutions are concerned, we tried walking a tightrope between the one extreme of assuming no changes during the next half century and the other of introducing technological breakthroughs or dramatic changes in tastes and institutions. The first alternative is far too unrealistic, while the second would have permitted us to prove anything we wanted. Instead, we chose a conservative approach that, so far as technology is concerned, assumes that labor productivity will grow more or less on trend, that substitutions of materials—for example, plastics for metals in certain uses—that are already taking place will continue, and that what is now considered best practice in one industry will become average practice by the year 2000. Tastes were handled in a similar fashion, the slow trend toward services being continued. Institutions were assumed to remain unchanged, except in specified circumstances where we wanted to assess the effects of special policies.

Finally, we studied these scenarios in two ways, first using a mathematical model of the economy modified to reflect the resource and environmental items under study, and second comparing these results with those obtained from more detailed studies of specific sectors, such as agriculture and energy. The final outcome represents a mixture of the results from these two approaches.

ARE WE "RUNNING OUT" OF RESOURCES?

Anyone who has studied this question even briefly knows that it is framed badly. An economy never completely runs out of anything.

When shortages threaten, prices rise, inducing increased supplies and choking off demand. But this way of posing the question is a convenient shorthand that captures the concern that many feel about the long-run consequences of population growth.

Our principal conclusion with respect to the population and economic growth assumptions investigated is that the United States is unlikely to experience any serious shortages during the next 30 to 50 years. By serious, we mean a situation in which the relative price of a large number of minerals and fuels rises by more than about 50 percent during this period of time. Factors other than population and economic growth may arise and threaten us with serious shortages. Environmental groups may refuse to permit the construction of sufficient nuclear electric plants or the Organization of Petroleum Exporting Countries may successfully impose monopolistic control over a large fraction of the world's petroleum supplies, and so on. But strictly as a consequence of population and economic growth in this country and the rest of the world, the United States is likely to be able to find the necessary supplies to meet rising demands without price rises of such a magnitude that the general welfare is endangered.

This finding is explained by the fact that we can see relatively simple ways to overcome potential shortages without assuming dramatic discoveries or technological breakthroughs. On the supply side, substitutes, recycling, and the mining of lower-grade ores would occur on a significantly increased scale if the price were to rise somewhat. On the demand side, a similar price rise would induce the use of substitutes, economies in use, institutional reorganization, and changes in tastes that would help close the gap. The automobile is a good example. Just imagine for a moment the many simple adjustments people would make if the automobile threatened to eat up a significantly larger portion of their personal budgets. In more technical language, there is reason to believe that the long-run supply and demand curves for most resources are fairly elastic.

This conclusion must be qualified in several ways. The United States will become somewhat more dependent on imports. We are assuming that prices act as appropriate signaling devices, indicating probable shortages sufficiently far in advance to allow time for corrective actions. And, of course, as indicated, we are not taking into account a wide variety of external factors that could arise during the next half century to upset this projection. Subject to these qualifications, our relatively sanguine conclusion with respect to the effects of population and economic growth on resources during the next 30 to 50 years stands.

THE RELATIVE IMPORTANCE
OF POPULATION

This is not to say that a slowdown in population growth would not ease whatever problems are likely to arise. Resource requirements, emission of pollutants into the environment, congestion, and risks of not being able to resolve problems through technological or institutional changes would all be somewhat less if the population were to cease growing. But how important is population growth, relative to the other causes of these problems?

In large part, the answer depends upon the time frame being considered. The longer the time horizon, the more important is population growth; the shorter the time period, the more important are other factors, such as tastes and public policies with respect to such common property resources as air and water. The answer also depends on the specific items being considered. In our studies, we found that population played its most important role with respect to pressures on land and water. Next in line come those things that heavily depend on land and water, such as the availability of outdoor recreation facilities and agricultural output. Although still important, population growth appears to be somewhat less responsible for pollution and resource shortages.

Figure 10-1 is fairly typical of the results obtained for many pollutants and resources. Taking a 30-year time period, it describes the amount of hydrocarbons that is likely to be generated and emitted under alternative assumptions about the rate of population growth, the rate of growth in per capita output, two technological alternatives, and two different policy regimes. The high-population-growth assumption corresponds roughly to an assumption that the average number of children per family is three; the low-population-growth assumption substitutes an average of two children per family. The high-economic-growth case assumes that the rate of decline of one-quarter of 1 percent per year in the average number of hours worked continues on trend. This assumption would bring weekly hours down from approximately 40 to 37 by the year 2000. In the low-economic-growth case, working hours per week are assumed to drop by 1 percent per year, which could mean working 29 hours per week by the year 2000.

The bars labeled A in Figure 10-1 indicate the amount of hydrocarbons generated by different economic activities, assuming no change in technology between 1970 and 2000. Comparing the bars in 2000, it

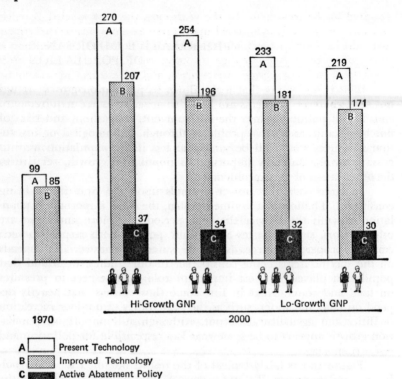

Figure. 10-1. Hydrocarbon emissions, in millions of pounds.

can be seen that a reduction in population growth would be somewhat less effective than a reduction in economic growth in reducing the level of hydrocarbons in that year,* but that in any event the levels would be much higher than those experienced today if there were no change in policy.

Bar B for 1970 indicates the amount of hydrocarbons actually emitted into the atmosphere; the difference between A and B is ac-

* This is true even when we compare the effects on pollution (and use of resources) of a 1 percent decline in population with the same decline in GNP per capita in the year 2000. There are several explanations, the more important being that if population were less in 2000, GNP per capita would be somewhat greater, assuming full employment is maintained in all cases. The increase in the latter partially offsets the beneficial effect of the reduction in population. On the other hand, if GNP per capita were to be less due to a slowdown in the growth of labor productivity, there would not be any necessarily offsetting change in population size.

counted for by treatment. In the year 2000, the bars labeled B reflect our estimate of emissions based upon three assumptions: (1) treatment per unit of hydrocarbons generated remains more or less the same as in 1970, (2) there is no change in policy with respect to the environment from the base period (1967–1970), and (3) changes in technology and production processes that would have come along anyway are permitted to play a role. Technological changes were introduced by assuming that the most efficient plants of 1970 become the average in the year 2000. Apparently, on net, technological changes of this sort will move in a cleaner direction even without pressures from environmental policy, but not fast enough to keep pollution from rising over current levels during this 30-year period.

The bars labeled C indicate what emission levels might be in the year 2000 if a "clean environment policy" were to be imposed. To simulate this policy, we applied the Environmental Protection Agency's suggested 1975 emission standards for various pollutants to our estimates of pollution generation levels for 2000. This is a conservative (thus, high) estimate of emission levels for that year. In fact, in most cases, we think the standards could be met in the near future if modest institutional changes as well as technological changes were considered.

As can be seen, the role of environmental policy is crucial: the various population and economic growth assumptions all result in significantly higher levels of hydrocarbon emissions, while the implementation of appropriate emission standards reduces the amount of pollutants to well below current levels. Moreover, a change in policy would not be excessively expensive. For the set of pollutants investigated, costs of treatment were about 1 percent of Gross National Product in 1970; they would amount to no more than 2 percent of GNP in the year 2000. Such a rate of expenditure would be equivalent to giving up less than one-tenth of 1 percent in annual growth of GNP.

The principal conclusion emerging from this figure, then, is that direct attacks on pollution problems clearly and easily dominate over reductions in population and economic growth as a strategy for obtaining a cleaner environment. It is reinforced by looking at local problems. Variations in pollution levels from city to city—indeed from area to area within a given city and from hour to hour at given locations—are so large that specialized local treatment of the problem will be needed no matter what national policies are adopted with respect to abatement, population, and economic growth. A reduction in population growth to zero, for example, would do virtually nothing about the amount of hydrocarbons along our principal arteries during rush hours.

Of course, this conclusion holds only for the 30-year period investigated. The longer the time period, the more effective would be a reduction in population growth. A potentially serious qualification to our findings concerns the exclusion from our study of other environmental pressures arising from population growth. For the most part, our study is limited to the widespread pollutants associated with industry, transport, and households. Pollutants that are smaller, but perhaps more toxic in amount, such as heavy metals, radiation, and pesticides, plus such environmental hazards as loss of genetic variability in plant stock, were handled in a much more cursory fashion. The problem here is the inability to quantify the relationship between population and economic activities on the one side and the environmental threat on the other. We know that the longer population and economic growth continues, the greater is the risk of serious environmental problems caused by these pollutants and hazards, but we do not know how much greater the risk is. Moreover, we can generally say less about the ability of policy and technological changes to cope with these threats.

SOCIAL AND INSTITUTIONAL PRESSURES

An exclusive focus on resource and environmental problems—on the "running out" type of questions—misses what might be the most important consequence of population growth: change in the character of society. Resource and environmental problems tend to be transformed into social and institutional pressures. In the process of adjusting to such problems, society will change in ways that many of us will not like.

The social and institutional costs of population growth may take four forms. The first involves a more contrived and regulated way of life, resulting from the need to ration increasingly scarce common property resources, such as public land, air, and water. Our projections of water demands and supplies, for example, indicate that at current prices more and more regions of the country will be threatened with shortages. This does not mean that catastrophe looms ahead of us as some writers suggest. There are many ways to alleviate these shortages, including building additional storage facilities, enacting more stringent regulation of waste emissions, increasing charges to reduce consumption, transferring population and economic activities to other regions, and constructing longer and larger canals to import water from surplus regions. But all these efforts require greater public interference in private decision making: the increase in taxes and regulations; the closing off of water bodies from easy, private access; the imposition of charges for what was once considered a free good; and so on. In many small ways we can expect population growth to add to the amount of red tape, bureaucracy, and queueing that governs our lives.

The second form involves the likelihood of continued postponement of solutions to fundamental social problems because increasingly greater efforts must be devoted to solving the resource and environmental problems thrown up by growth. Limited research funds, capital, managerial skills, and trained manpower *must* be devoted to finding new sources of energy, designing motor engines that emit less pollutants, devising ways to recycle wastes, and planning more effective regulatory systems. Less talent—in terms of both quantity and quality—is likely to be left for work on race relations, crime, drugs, mass transit, housing, and so on.

For similar reasons, we may be forced to introduce solutions to pending problems before all the side-effects are known. It may, for example, be far better environmentally to bypass the construction of nuclear fission plants and wait until the inherently cleaner and safer fusion process is developed, but the projected demand for electricity appears to be making this impossible. Similarly, we do not understand all the ecological consequences of the massive water projects we will have to undertake in the next half century.

Finally, all such changes result in closing off options for alternative life styles. As population density increases, wilderness areas recede, resources become less abundant, and dependence on continued technological change grows, slow but irreversible changes in our current way of life are forced upon us. Some may like these changes, but for those who do not, there will be fewer options.

SOME POLICY IMPLICATIONS

To summarize, we have found that further population growth in the United States during the next 30 to 50 years would yield no advantages and entail some costs. These costs involve a somewhat more rapid depletion of domestic and international resources, greater pressures on the environment, more dependence on continued rapid technological development, greater risks, and a number of potentially serious social and institutional costs. As long as population growth continues, these problems will grow, slowly but irreversibly forcing changes in our current way of life. If population growth were to cease, we would purchase time, resources, and additional options: time to overcome our ignorance and to redress the mistakes of past growth, resources to implement solutions, and additional freedom of choice in deciding how we want to live in the future.

The presence of social costs arising from population growth suggest that we should at least eliminate all pronatalist biases in current legislation and institutions. Just how far we should go toward antinatalism depends on the weight we give to private preferences relative to social costs. Fortunately, at this stage in our history, the norm in private preferences seem to be moving toward small families. Because of this, legislative changes, other than those necessary to provide individuals with as much free choice as possible to implement their preferences, may be unnecessary at the present time. But given the historic variability in such preferences, the situation requires continuous monitoring.

Should economic growth also be stopped or at least slowed down? Here, it is necessary to differ sharply from those who advocate zero economic growth as well as zero population growth. It is true that many of the consequences of continued economic growth are similar to those of population growth. Indeed, as Figure 10-1 indicates, a reduction in economic growth would reduce pollution emissions by more than would a comparable reduction in population. The same is true for resource consumption. But growth in the economy can be used for different ends than it is put to now. Although it adds to the problems that need solution, it also adds to the capacity to solve problems. This is another way of indicating the importance of direct attacks on resource and environmental problems. In effect, these attacks force a change in the composition of output, one that permits almost the same amount of economic growth to continue, but in a far less damaging way.

But what about problems lying beyond the half-century time horizon of our study? And what about the environmental threats we have not been able to analyze in detail, some of which are believed by ecologists to be more threatening than the ones we have analyzed? These are areas where ignorance dominates. Should we not, in effect, stop the train, or at least slow it down, until we know more about what is around the bend? Once again, so far as population growth is concerned, there is no disagreement: we simply cannot find any social advantages to further population growth. But per capita economic growth is another thing altogether.

It is true that we may not know what kind of disasters we may be letting ourselves in for by permitting economic growth to continue. But it should be remembered that we are also ignorant of possible technological and institutional breakthroughs that may come along eventually, breakthroughs that might not only save future generations from disaster, but also make them substantially better off than the current generation. In the light of total ignorance about both positive and negative developments that may occur, what is the prudent course? It is not obvious that it consists in saving resources for future generations.

The analogy of stopping the train until one knows what is around the corner is an interesting one, conjuring up a picture of passengers sitting comfortably in lounge cars until railroad personnel inspect the tracks ahead. It is a rich man's image. The poorer two-thirds of the world's population cannot wait, particularly when it is not clear that future generations will be worse off than people today. If we want the poor to wait, the prudent course would be to share the lounge chair—that is, the available resources—with them.

These general conclusions follow only if we do in fact take advantage of the opportunities available to attack environmental and resource problems directly. If political and institutional constraints make it impossible to apply direct measures very forcefully, we are likely, as Figure 10-1 shows, to have much higher levels of pollution in the future. In that situation, reductions in economic as well as population growth begin to make more sense. Those who advocate reductions in both types of growth may believe that we will not apply direct measures with sufficient force. I hope we can prove them wrong.

REFERENCES

BRUBAKER, STERLING. 1972. *To Live on Earth.* Baltimore: Johns Hopkins Press for Resources for the Future.

COMMISSION ON POPULATION GROWTH AND THE AMERICAN FUTURE. 1972. *Population, Resources, and the Environment,* Ronald G. Ridker, ed. Research Reports of the Commission on Population Growth and the American Future, Vol. 3. Washington: U.S. Government Printing Office. See especially Part I, "Resource and Environmental Consequences of Population Growth in the United States."

ROBERT PARKE ==

11. *The Impact of Population Growth on Government and Society*

To explore the question of population impacts on government, we must first specify the aspects of population change and the aspects of government whose connections we wish to examine, then choose formal or informal models that relate the two. In speaking of population, we must, of course, include the total numbers of people, rates of change, and the associated shifts in age composition. Beyond this, we may also want to look at *how* the changes occur—whether by changes in mortality, fertility, or migration, or by the evolving impact of the age structure on these processes. It may also be productive to go beyond the effects of national population growth in the aggregate and take account of the form in which the growth occurs—such as the decline of rural areas and the dominance of metropolitan areas or such compositional changes as racial, sex, educational, occupational, and family size distribution—and the way these affect the character of the society.

With respect to government, we may focus on federal, state, or local levels or on various governmental functions, such as taxation, national defense, the administration of justice, and the provision of such services as education, health, and welfare. We may focus on the structure, interrelations, and functions of governing bodies or extend

Robert Parke is director of the Center for Coordination of Research on Social Indicators of the Social Science Research Council. He has served as deputy director of the Commission on Population Growth and the American Future and with the U.S. Bureau of the Census.

our concern to include the processes of public opinion, citizen participation, interest group conflict, shifting political party affiliation, and
the general liberalism or conservatism of the society.

Then there is the question of models. Broadly, a model refers to
one's conception of government's key parts and how they work and
one's conception of the role of government in the society at large.
Whatever framework is adopted, two decisions must be made: What
influences other than population and government are to be introduced
into the analysis? Are we to treat government simply as a dependent
variable subject to population influence or acknowledge its interactions with population?

The governmental research of the Commission on Population
Growth and the American Future, although not definitive, dealt with
these issues comprehensively. It defined both population and government broadly for purposes of analysis. In addition, the models for
development of the research viewed government not only as a set of
institutions and processes subject to change as a result of population
change, but also as having large, if inadvertent, effects on population
trends and a potentially large activist role in modifying trends.

GOVERNMENT COSTS

The Population Commission organized its research around a
simple question. It said to its researchers, "Suppose that between now
and the year 2000 the population grows at a rate consistent with an
average family size of two children. Suppose, on the other hand, that
population growth occurs at a rate consistent with an average of three
children per family. What difference would it make?" The question
was addressed to demographers, sociologists, economists, resource ex-
perts, ecologists, political scientists, and others. Each was asked to
describe, from the point of view of his specialty, the consequences of
the two-child versus the three-child projection.

The levels selected for study were the high and low projections
available from the U.S. Census Bureau. Either projected level is
plausible. Each has actually been achieved by groups of American
women in the twentieth century. In 1970, fertility averaged between
2.4 and 2.5 children per woman.

Several of the studies projected the government costs associated
with the two-child and three-child rates of future population growth.
Costs in three areas were examined—health, education, and welfare
(Appleman et al., in press). These are services to people and therefore,
are presumed to be more directly sensitive to changes in population

than other activities such as fire protection, road building, and general administration. Education costs, the studies showed, would be far less under the two-child than under the three-child growth rate. Assume that in the future schools upgrade their quality, and enrollment rates rise fairly rapidly. In the year 2000, the education bill for a two-child population would amount to 9.7 percent of the gross national product, or $276 billion. The corresponding costs for a three-child population would be 13 percent of GNP, or over $400 billion. In 1970, the figures were 7.5 percent of GNP, or $74 billion, but the projections assume an improvement in quality. There are substantial trade-offs between the quality of future education and its quantity. Suppose that 10 percent of GNP were allocated to education in the year 2000. In a three-child population this would buy a 1970 quality of education for 93 percent of students and a superior quality for only 7 percent. In the two-child population, this amount of money would permit all students to receive a superior quality of education, equivalent to the best contemporary standards of teaching personnel, methods, and equipment.

The commission's research on welfare and health costs associated with different future rates of population growth produced no such results. The reasons for this are instructive, as we shall see. For purposes of this research, welfare costs were not measured directly. Rather, we sought to determine the effects of the two-child versus the three-child growth rate on *welfare needs*, which we defined as the amount of money that would have to be spent to bring all family incomes up to a poverty line established by the government. By this definition, welfare needs exceed current welfare expenditures by a large amount. Nonetheless, so long as the discussion is kept on a consistent footing, this definition will serve.

Experience shows that public notions of how much the poor need rise with the general level of affluence, but not as fast. If per capita income in the United States continues to rise, the official definition of poverty is not likely to remain fixed at its present dollar level. On the other hand, the official definition is not likely to rise as fast as per capita income. For purposes of projecting welfare needs, both the constant and the relative definitions of poverty were used, on the assumption that what actually transpires will fall somewhere in between.

Using either definition, the results show that the welfare needs of a two-child population in the year 2000 would not differ very much from those of a three-child population—not more than $2 billion, according to these estimates, and probably less. Relative to GNP in the year 2000, this amount would be insignificant. This is the result we get when using a constant poverty definition. Upward shifts in the income distribution, associated with the economic growth that is expected by the year 2000, will leave relatively few families below today's poverty income standard—so few that projected differences in the number of poor people produced by differences in the number of children are trivial in absolute terms.

Using a relative poverty standard, the projected welfare need is naturally much larger, but it is probably not much different in the two-child than in the three-child population. This result contradicts our common-sense expectations and thus bears examination. What is going on? For one thing, when we define poverty in relative terms, we set a higher standard for a two-child population. As Stephen Enke's paper in this volume points out, per capita income is expected to increase faster under conditions of slower population growth (see Chapter 9). This effect is due largely to the fact that the number of dependents will not rise as fast as the number of producers, with the result that a given amount of income is shared by fewer people. Higher per capita income under conditions of slower population growth is also expected to result from the larger proportion of women expected in the labor force under conditions of low fertility.

Obviously, if poverty is defined relative to per capita income, the more affluent society will set a higher standard. On this score, the conclusion of the research may be restated by saying that it will not cost the slower-growing population any less to eliminate poverty, because such a population is expected to define poverty in more generous terms. In the words of the researchers, "the smaller number of households and the reduction in household size associated with slower population growth are offset by the more rapid rate of increase in per capita income and hence in the relative poverty threshold." Such a result really confirms our intuitive expectation that slower population growth would help in the reduction of poverty.

There is another reason for the unexpected result of this research and that is that most poor families do not have children. Again, the researchers write: "Only about one out of three poor households includes children; a lower birthrate cannot have much effect on the poverty threshold or the poverty gap facing a childless family." In fact, the aged, not the young, have the highest poverty rates of any age group, with the result that their proportion of the poor is about twice their proportion in the population (10 percent of Americans are 65 and over). But the number of aged will not be affected by future birthrates; everybody who will be over 30 in the year 2000 was already alive in 1970. Since half the people in poverty are over 30, the effect that population changes can have on welfare needs between now and the year 2000 is substantially muted.

As for health care, the commission reported,

We looked at the demand for physician visits, dental visits, and hospital beds. We found that, for a given quality of health care, the more rapidly growing population would spend $20 billion more over the next three decades than would the slower growing population. This averages out to a difference in annual expenditure of less than $1 billion (Commission . . . , 1972, p. 55).

The age pattern of health care and the demography of population change combine to produce this result. Except for dental visits, utilization of all forms of health care rises with age (National Center for Health Statistics, 1970). This rise is especially rapid for hospital care, both of the long-term and short-term variety, and it also applies to physician visits. Differences in birthrates over the next 30 years cannot have much effect on the number of people who will make heavy use of health services in the year 2000.

There is a lesson in the results of this analysis. The reductions in mortality that have given us a life expectancy in excess of 70 years have slowed change in our population. The year 2000 is a long way beyond almost anyone's planning horizon. But 30 years is not a long time for changes in a long-lived population such as ours. We stop our analysis at the year 2000 because we know too little beyond that to conjure up plausible scenarios for health, education, and welfare services, or for much else. But in restricting our analysis to the remainder of this century, we must expect only effects that can be caused by changes in the younger half of the population. Accordingly, we find major effects for education, minor effects for welfare, and negligible effects for health care.

Because the costs of health, education, and welfare are borne mainly by states and localities, a full understanding of how these and other governmental costs will be affected by population change requires that we go below the studies of national aggregates described above (Drury, 1972; Grumm, 1973). The gravest disparities are found within metropolitan areas. While suburbs attract the more affluent, the major cities are left with disproportionate numbers of children, the poor, and the aged. The cities have both a greater demand for services and a population that is less capable of paying the bill. The unequal effect is illustrated in Louisville, where the city has less than half the population of the metropolitan area, but over 90 percent of the area's welfare recipients.

NATIONAL SECURITY, CONGRESSIONAL
REPRESENTATION, AND JUSTICE

In the area of national security, the uniform judgment of the many scholars and government officials we consulted was that the manpower needs of the military would be amply supplied in a two-child population (Commission . . . , 1972, pp. 58–59). Although this is chiefly the result of the high reliance of the U.S. military on technological development, it is also partly a legacy of the baby boom: even though a two-child average is lower than recent fertility levels, the number of people of childbearing age will increase so much over the next decade that projections that assume a steady two-child average show no year between now and the year 2000 in which the number of births would be lower than they were in 1971. In reality, whatever happens to fertility, it will not happen steadily. We will have fluctuations. Still, the point remains that the population of the United States has a high potential for future growth, higher than that of any other advanced country. If this is a cause for dismay on many other grounds, it is, by the same token, a source of reassurance for those concerned about military manpower.

The commission's research on representation in Congress showed that since 1911, when the size of the House of Representatives was fixed at 435 members, the average population of a congressional district has risen from 211,000 to 470,000 in 1970. In the year 2000, the average size would be 623,000 in a two-child population and 741,000 in a three-child population. Electronics and air travel have, of course, improved the ability of congressmen to communicate with their constituents. However, it is not clear that there have been equivalent improvements in the individual constituent's ability to communicate with congressmen.

If the difference between the number of constituents per congressman under the two-child and three-child assumptions does not appear very large, it must be remembered that the projected future populations are points in a trajectory and that the ultimate difference would be far greater. A rapidly growing population does not have the option of suddenly stopping its growth. The legacy of the baby boom is but one demonstration of the fact that future population growth is largely determined by a population's past history of growth. "We may be through with the past," said the commission, "but the past is not done with us." Continuation of a three-child average for a century would produce a population of nearly a billion Americans in the year 2070, and the average congressman would have triple the number of constituents he would have had in a two-child population. Even if technical wonders produced vast improvements in communication, it is hard to believe it would not be a very different body under these circumstances, as it has become a very different body in this century—more hierarchical in organization, more careerist and more specialized with respect to the participation of its members, and more routinized in the conduct of daily business in order to accommodate the staggering increase in workload (Davidson, 1972). There were 268 bills introduced in the first Congress and nearly 25,000 in the ninety-first; laws enacted rose from 118 to 909, presidential messages from 12 to 285, and committee reports from 155 to 3,355. As Speaker Joe Martin once said, "Nowadays bills which 30 years ago would have been thrashed out for hours or days go through in ten minutes . . ." (Davidson, 1972). Competing with the congressman's responsibilities as a member of a collegial lawmaking body come increased demands from constituents for attention to their problems or complaints.

Although the executive branch may adapt to an increased workload by increasing its size, its specialization, its routines, or its hierarchy, Congress cannot adapt very far in these directions without losing its collegial character and its openness to influence from outside sources.

Far more is involved, of course, than the sheer increase in the number of constituents. A congressman now has a far better educated, more informed, more critical, and more demanding constituency, whose expectations have been shaped in an era of big government. Such qualitative changes, it has been asserted, have done more than the increase in population numbers to raise the demands made of Congress (Davidson, 1972). Yet the overall effect is a product of numbers of constituents times their per capita demands taken together. One multiplies the other to produce the total impact. If smart, critical citizens with big expectations make such demands as to endanger the ability of Congress to respond, surely more such citizens do not make the problem any easier.

The backlog of cases in the nation's courts is well known. In the District of Columbia, the situation is so critical that in 1970 the Chief Justice was moved to describe it as "little short of disaster." The Supreme Court recently reduced the time allowed for oral arguments from two hours to one hour, in the chamber where Daniel Webster once argued the Dartmouth College case for several days.

A commission researcher attributed this situation to two factors: (1) the fondness an increasingly urban population has for legal battles, and (2) the increasing deference to due process over the past decade, in contrast to the "crime control" approach to justice, with its high percentage of guilty pleas in criminal cases, out-of-court settlements of civil suits, and so forth (Vines, 1972). Other demographic developments have also contributed to the crisis in the courts by increasing the number of cases brought to their attention:

> Since the crime rate is higher among persons under 25 than among older people, much of the increase in crime during recent years is traceable to an expansion in the relative number of persons in the youthful age groups. About 28 percent of the reported increase between 1960 and 1970 in the number of arrests for serious crimes can be attributed to an increase in the percentage of the population under 25. Another 22 percent of the increase can be explained by the growing size of the population and other demographic factors. Thus, population change alone accounted for about half of the reported increase in the number of arrests for serious crimes over the past decade (Commission . . . , 1972, pp. 19 & 22).

If crime is a greater problem in metropolitan areas than elsewhere, one reason is the extraordinary increase in the age groups that are most productive of what the FBI classifies as serious crime. Between 1960 and 1970, the number of white youths 15–24 years old in metropolitan areas outside the South increased by half and the number of black youths doubled (Taeuber, in press).

GOVERNMENT AS PART OF THE PROBLEM

I have reviewed several ways in which population change affects government. It must also be acknowledged that powerful influences work in the opposite direction. For example, government affects population directly through immigration policies, abortion laws, and public health programs to reduce mortality. It affects population indirectly through tax laws and subsidization of education.

There is another important way in which government fits into the picture. If we accept that the influence that factor x has on factor y depends on the state of some factor z (as, for example, the influence of atmospheric moisture on the chances of precipitation depends on temperature), then we may ask in what ways government affects the relationship between population and anything that is affected by population. Articulating this viewpoint, the commission said:

> Population change does not take place in a vacuum. Its consequences are produced through its joint action with technology, wealth, and the institutional structures of society. Hence, a study of the American future, insofar as it is influenced by population change, cannot ignore,

indeed it must comment upon, the features of the society that make population growth troublesome or not (Commission . . . , 1972, p. 77).

The obsolescence of government institutions is clearly one of the things that makes the growth of a large, rich, high-technology population troublesome. This is nowhere clearer than when we look at the difficulties that inherited structures of local government pose for the management of modern metropolitan communities.

Metropolitan population growth is the form that national population growth has taken and will continue to take. This growth occurs irrespective of the political boundaries of townships, counties, and municipalities large and small. The result is that many jurisdictions, with differing burdens and differing resources, find themselves part of the same territorial and economic community, but without adequate means of handling community-wide affairs.

The most unsettling projection prepared for the Population Commission was not a population projection. It was a projection of the number of local governments in metropolitan areas in the United States (Manvel, 1972). Not counting school districts, which have been consolidating, there were 16,000 local government units in metropolitan areas in 1970. If recent trends continue, the number will double to 32,000 by the year 2000. The proliferation of specialized districts with independent revenue-raising and policy-making powers will account for half the increase. Anyone who thinks we have problems now with environmental management, land-use planning, urban transportation, residential segregation, and overburdened central city governments should ponder the implications of these figures. Moreover, the fragmentation of local government can be traced directly to the actions of higher governmental levels. The encouragement of incorporation and discouragement of annexation by state governments created suburban exclusiveness, and federal housing programs have implicitly endorsed it (Danielson, 1972).

AGING AND SOCIETY

A distinctive feature of a stationary population is its relative abundance of old people and its relative scarcity of youth. Under contemporary American conditions of mortality, a population in which births equalled deaths would have virtually as many 15-year-olds as 50-year-olds. In 1970, however, 15-year-olds outnumbered 50-year-olds by nearly two to one. These observations have given rise to a good deal of speculation, most of it tinged with anxiety, about the social consequences of an aging population (Day, 1972).

It has been suggested that increasing proportions of the aged would burden the society with dependents, yet it is clear that *total* dependency—youth as well as aged—would be less in a stationary population than in a growing one. Persons over 65 and under 18, who comprised 44 percent of the population in 1970, would comprise only 40 percent in a stationary population under present mortality conditions. Although the population over 65 would rise from 10 to 16 percent of the total, those under 18 would decline from 34 to 24 percent (Commission . . . , 1972, p. 62).

The significance of age is partly dependent on the meaning given to it by culture and institutions. In Sweden people retire at 70, in India at 55. A society with high longevity is likely to be a society in which health and vitality are preserved into fairly advanced years, and where active involvement of old people is feasible, if custom will only define it as permissible and desirable.

The concern over whether a stationary population age structure would tend to produce "social stagnation" seems to rest on three ideas. One is the observation that older people are more conservative than youth. Related to this is the observation that innovation and social change operate partly through the succession of generations. The third is the hypothesis that the career mobility of youth would be slowed in a stationary population because of the abundance of senior citizens filling the top jobs.

It is not at all clear that relatively high proportions of old people tend to produce a conservative society. Sweden is progressive in many respects, yet its age structure is not much different from the one we would have if our population were stationary. The other reasons for concern remain to be demonstrated. They are important, they are researchable, and they deserve scientific investigation, preferably by a mathematical sociologist. It should be noted, however, that the succession of generations occurs most rapidly in populations with short lifetimes and high rates of reproduction, that is, in the most traditional societies in the world. The value placed on youth in the United States is associated with their scarcity, not with their abundance. The small generation of Depression babies did very well in the job market, but the children of the baby boom are having a harder time. We confuse the influence of youth with their visibility, which results from their prominence in the consumer goods market and the frequency with which they are arrested. But their influence in affairs and their prospects for advancement depend on their possession of scarce skills. With new occupations and skills multiplying, it is difficult to see how making youth relatively scarce can work to their detriment. If it works to their advantage, it means they will be catered to, and if that happens, what grounds have we to worry that the aged will be dominant or youth immobilized?

REFERENCES

APPLEMAN, JACK; BUTZ, WILLIAM P.; GREENBERG, DAVID H.; JORDAN, PAUL L.; & PASCAL, ANTHONY. In press. "Population Change and Public Resource Requirements." In *Economic Aspects of Population Change*, R. H. Reed & E. R. Morss, eds. Research Reports of the Commission on Population Growth and the American Future, Vol. 2. Washington: U.S. Government Printing Office.

COMMISSION ON POPULATION GROWTH AND THE AMERICAN FUTURE. 1972. *Population and the American Future: Report of the Commission.* Washington: U.S. Government Printing Office.

DANIELSON, MICHAEL N. 1972. "Differentiation, Segregation, and Political Fragmentation in the American Metropolis." In *Governance and Population: The Governmental Implications of Population Change*, A. E. K. Nash, ed. Research Reports of the Commission on Population Growth and the American Future, Vol. 4. Washington: U.S. Government Printing Office, pp. 143–76.

DAVIDSON, ROGER H. 1972. "Population Change and Representative Government." In *Governance and Population: The Governmental Implications of Population Change*, A. E. K. Nash, ed. Research Reports of the Commission on Population Growth and the American Future, Vol. 4. Washington: U.S. Government Printing Office, pp. 59–82.

DAY, LINCOLN H. 1972. "The Social Consequences of a Zero Population Growth Rate in the United States." In *Demographic and Social Aspects of Population Growth*, Charles F. Westoff & Robert Parke, Jr., eds. Research Reports of the Commission on Population Growth and the American Future, Vol. 1. Washington: U.S. Government Printing Office, pp. 659–74.

DRURY, ROBERT F. 1972. "Local Governments and Population Change." In *Governance and Population: The Governmental Implications of Population Change*, A. E. K. Nash, ed. Research Reports of the Commission on Population Growth and the American Future, Vol. 4. Washington: U.S. Government Printing Office, pp. 109–24.

GRUMM, JOHN G. 1973. "Population Change and State Government Policy." In *Governance and Population: The Governmental Implications of Population Change*, A. E. K. Nash, ed. Research Reports of the Commission on Population Growth and the American Future, Vol. 4. Washington: U.S. Government Printing Office, pp. 125–41.

MANVEL, ALLEN D. 1972. "Metropolitan Growth and Governmental Fragmentation." In *Governance and Population: The Governmental Im-*

plications of Population Change, A. E. K. Nash, ed. Research Reports of the Commission on Population and the American Future, Vol. 4. Washington: U.S. Government Printing Office, pp. 177–216.

NATIONAL CENTER FOR HEALTH STATISTICS. 1970. "Age Patterns in Medical Care, Illness, and Disability, United States, 1968–1969." In *Vital and Health Statistics,* Series 10, no. 70 (April 1970).

TAEUBER, IRENE B. In press. "The Changing Distribution of the Population of the United States in the Twentieth Century." In *Population Distribution and Policy,* S. M. Mazie, ed. Research Reports of the Commission on Population Growth and the American Future, Vol. 5. Washington: U.S. Government Printing Office.

VINES, KENNETH N. 1972. "Population Increase and the Administration of Justice." In *Governance and Population: The Governmental Implications of Population Change,* A. E. K. Nash, ed. Research Reports of the Commission on Population Growth and the American Future, Vol. 4. Washington: U.S. Government Printing Office, pp. 217–228.

12. Perfect Fertility Control: Consequences for Women and the Family

It would seem that perfect fertility control in the United States is within reach, given the effectiveness of modern contraceptive methods and the recent Supreme Court ruling that permits abortion on request. But we are far from such an achievement. This is hardly because of a lack of knowledge about birth control, nor can we say that it is simply the unavailability of methods. A very important constraint is insufficient motivation. The level of motivation to control fertility is determined by numerous social, economic, and cultural factors. Accordingly, many changes in our society must come first if we are ever to achieve perfect fertility control. But we are moving in this direction, and it is interesting to speculate about the consequences. In this chapter, we are specifically interested in considering what perfect fertility control will mean for women and the family. Our focus on the consequences and not the determinants minimizes the extent to which the two interact. For example, while changes in the roles of women may motivate women to practice effective fertility control, at the same time the prac-

Harriet B. Presser is an associate professor of sociomedical science in the School of Public Health at Columbia University and a member of the International Institute for the Study of Human Reproduction. She formerly worked for the Population Council, where she specialized in the study of the social and demographic aspects of sterilization.

The author would like to express her thanks to Ruth Dixon, Sue Teper, and David Eversley for critically reading this paper during its preparation.

tice of effective fertility control may bring about changes in the roles of women. Recognizing that our focus is limited, we shall consider the following hypothetical question: if all persons in our society who would like to control their fertility were to do so with 100 percent effectiveness, what would the consequences be for women and the family? To explore this question, we need first to consider the consequences with respect to fertility.

THE DECLINE IN FERTILITY

Perfect fertility control would mean that fecund couples could have as many or as few children as they want. Although this does not necessarily mean a decline in fertility, we would expect this to be so for the United States today. Even in the late 1960s, it was conservatively estimated that 2.65 million births would never have occurred between 1965 and 1970 had all couples who did not want additional children practiced contraception with perfect efficiency (Commission . . . , 1972).

We are referring here to "unwanted" fertility, technically referred to as "number failures." These are births that occurred after the desired family size had been achieved. "Number failures" may be distinguished from "timing failures," which are births that were wanted later than they occurred. The proportion of all wanted births that are timing failures is substantial. Currently married couples in 1970 reported that over two-fifths of all their wanted births were timing failures.*

Although the practice of perfect fertility control would eventually eliminate both types of failures for all women, initially it would play a greater role among older women in eliminating number failures, and among younger women in eliminating timing failures. The impact of having fewer children may be quite different from the impact of planning the timing of births. Thus, in considering the impact of perfect fertility control on the roles of women, it is important to distinguish the two sources of change.

Before proceeding with such an analysis, it should be noted that we are not considering couples who would like to have children—or to have more children—but cannot because of fecundity problems. We are considering the majority of the population—fecund couples who wish to practice birth control. Moreover, it is recognized that, even

* Preliminary figures provided by the Office of Population Research at Princeton University.

with totally effective birth control practice, births cannot always be perfectly timed. Totally effective practice will only assure that children are not born *before* they are planned, but conception may still occur later than planned.

IMPACT OF SMALLER FAMILIES
ON THE ROLES OF WOMEN

What would the consequences be for women today if all who have achieved (or surpassed) their desired family size started to practice perfect fertility control? We indicated previously that this would mean a decline in family size, but how would having fewer children (assuming no change in the timing of births) affect the participation of women in social roles—both within the family as wives and mothers, and outside the family as students and employed workers?

The prevention of excess fertility would mean that women would be younger at the birth of the last child, as well as when their last child starts school, finishes school, and leaves home. Undoubtedly both familial and nonfamilial roles would be affected. Not only would certain aspects of the mother role be altered, but the nature of the wife role would be changed as well. Some have argued that the importance of the personal relationship between husband and wife may increase as families become smaller (Ridley, 1973). It would seem that women in particular would change their expectations of the marital relationship as they became less preoccupied with the raising of young children. Depending on the particular circumstances, marital relationships would improve or divorce would be sought more frequently.

Women may also turn increasingly to nonfamilial roles as a consequence of having smaller families. Some may choose to return to school and continue their education, but the more common response would be increased participation of young mothers in the labor force. Actually, this would represent only an acceleration of the current trend. Indeed, the greatest increase in female labor force participation over the past decade has been among young mothers. By 1969, close to half of all married women with children aged 6 to 17 years old (and no children under 6 years of age) were in the labor force; over one-fourth of married women with children of preschool age were working (Ferriss, 1971, Figure 7.13). The working woman has been very aptly referred to as "one of America's best kept secrets" (Keller, 1973) and this is particularly true of the working mother.

Although female labor force participation is expected to increase as a consequence of smaller families, there is no reason to expect that these women will hold better jobs than they held before starting their families: the sex-typing of jobs produces considerable stability in the kinds of jobs available to women. At this stage of their lives, these women are not as likely as younger women to press for change. Having married and had their children early, the change for them would be primarily one of financial independence, which may serve to improve their status within the family (Ridley, 1973). It may also precipitate divorce at this stage of their lives—whether desired by the husband, wife, or both—since it now becomes economically more feasible.

IMPACT OF THE PLANNED TIMING OF BIRTHS ON THE ROLES OF WOMEN

Initially, perfect fertility control would enable those who have achieved their desired number of children to avoid unwanted births and it would enable younger women to plan the timing of wanted births. Ultimately, women would have perfect control over both the timing and the number of births. Specifically, the ability to plan the first birth has the greatest potential for changing the roles of women. This becomes clear when we consider that, for most women, the timing of the first birth represents the onset of child care (and, for many, marriage itself). The transition from no children to one child is more critical than the change to any higher number of children, because having a first child generally has a far more restrictive effect on a woman's daily activities than having an additional child. Thus, as long as women bear the major responsibility for child care, the timing of the first birth has significant consequences for the rest of their lives (Presser, 1971).

If all first births were planned, this would affect the familial roles of women by eliminating most illegitimacy (assuming that most illegitimate births are unplanned) and "shotgun" weddings. Over 16 percent of all first births in 1968 were illegitimate (U.S. Dept. of Commerce, 1971b, Table 28). A recent government study estimated that of all legitimate first births occurring between 1964 and 1966, about one in five were premaritally conceived. For women aged 15 to 19, the ratio is over two in five (U.S. Dept. of Commerce, 1971b, Table 23). And, for all married women in 1970, over one-third report that their first births were timing failures.* The perfect planning of the first birth would mean for many women, then, the postponement

---

* Preliminary data provided by the Office of Population Research at Princeton University.

of marriage and motherhood, and, for some, remaining single and/or "child-free" forever.* Unfortunately, we do not know just how long women would wait before marrying or having their first child if they did not have timing failures. Indeed, women themselves may not be able to predict this accurately. They may not anticipate the impact of a delayed first birth on their behavior in nonfamilial roles, which in turn may change their plans for the timing of marriage and/ or motherhood.

For many women, not having the first child until it is wanted will mean more child-free time to continue their educations and acquire occupational interests and skills outside the home. Since the broadening of options outside the home may reduce a woman's desire to become a mother at all or to have many children, it should contribute to reducing family size.

Recent trends lend some support to these hypotheses. Data from the 1965 and 1970 National Fertility Studies reveal that highly effective contraceptive methods are becoming increasingly popular among young married women. Unfortunately, data from the 1970 National Fertility Study are not yet available that differentiate between the use of contraception before and after the first birth. But among married women who were under 30 in 1970, no matter how many children they had, close to 39 percent were using the pill or the IUD, as compared with slightly over 27 percent in 1965 (Westoff, 1972). This undoubtedly has had the effect of postponing the timing of the first birth. Census data for 1960 indicated that among women aged 20 to 24 who were or had been married, close to 25 percent had no children. By 1969 the proportion increased to over 34 percent (U.S. Dept. of Commerce, 1971b, Table 13). But even though there is apparently a postponement in the timing of legitimate first births, the trend in illegitimacy seems to be toward earlier timing. For women aged 15 to 19, the number of illegitimate births per 1,000 unmarried women rose from 15.3 in 1960 to 19.8 in 1968 (U.S. Dept. of Commerce, 1971b, Table 25). It may be that the increase in highly effective contraceptive practice prior to the first birth is specific to married women. Unmarried women may be engaging in sexual intercourse at an earlier age than in the past. It may also be that women who become pregnant before marriage (and do not have an induced abortion) are increasingly less likely to marry in order to legitimize the birth. When combining legitimate and illegitimate first births, there is a slight postponement in timing: the median age at first birth rose from 21.8 in 1960 to 22.1 in 1968 (U.S. Dept. of

* David Sills appropriately suggests that we refer to women without children as being "child-free" rather than "childless," since the latter term implies a negative status.

Health, Education and Welfare, 1971, Table 1-11). The age at first marriage for all women has also been rising in recent years, from a median of 20.3 in 1960 to 20.9 in 1971 (U.S. Dept. of Commerce, 1971a, Table C). This slight upward trend in the age at first marriage and at first birth represents a reversal in the trend toward younger ages that was characteristic of the postwar period up to about 1960.

Along with the overall postponement in the assumption of familial roles, there has been a change in the levels of participation of women in roles outside the family. Women are increasingly extending the number of years they remain in school. Although this is not a reversal of earlier trends (educational attainment has been rising for women since 1900), there was an accelerated increase in the number of women earning college degrees at the bachelor's, master's, and doctoral level after 1960 relative to the 1950s (Ferriss, 1971, Figure 3.8). The labor force participation rates of young women increased sharply in the 1960s as compared with the previous decade, when rates were relatively stable for women in their early twenties. In 1960, 44.9 percent of all women aged 20 to 24 were in the labor force (U.S. Dept. of Commerce, 1961, Table 1); by 1969, the percentage had risen to 56.8 (U.S. Dept. of Labor, 1970, Table A-2). Recent data are not yet available on the occupational status of women of different age groups, but if we compare the status of women of all ages in 1969 to that in 1960, some improvement can be seen. The percentage of working women in professional and kindred occupations, for example, was 12.2 in 1960 and 14.7 in 1969 (U.S. Dept. of Commerce, 1969, Table 322). The improvement in occupational status suggested by the total figures may become even more notable when we are able to consider only young women.

As young women have been participating more fully in roles outside the home, the number of children they expect to have has been declining. In 1967, married women aged 18 to 24 indicated that they expected, on the average, 2.9 children (U.S. Dept. of Commerce, 1971c). By 1971—only four years later—comparable women reported that they expected to have an average of 2.4 children (U.S. Dept. of Commerce, 1972).

These changes in the roles of young women and in their desired family size may well be a direct consequence of the increased use of effective contraception among young women in the 1960s—at least among the married women. This has enabled them to plan their births more effectively and, in turn, has given them more assurance of realizing their aspirations outside the family. If all births were planned, and most importantly the first birth, more women would benefit from increased child-free time and less childrearing time, and a growing proportion would pursue educational and occupational opportunities. Family-size desires, accordingly, would decline. This assumes, of course, that there would be opportunities for women—that sex discrimination and unfavorable economic conditions would not severely restrict the extent or level of female participation in roles outside the family. In other words, we are assuming that the rise in aspirations *and* in opportunities is concomitant.

THE DIVERSITY IN LIFE STYLES
AND FAMILY SIZE

Perfect fertility control does not suggest that all young women will wish to continue their education and seek careers outside the home. Rather, it means that more women than ever before will have time to consider the options and to experiment with them without unplanned interruptions. Such experimentation will reveal to some women that there are alternative sources of fulfillment aside from motherhood. Others may feel, on the basis of expectations or experience, that activities outside the home cannot be substitutes for the rewards of motherhood; they may want to be at home full-time raising a family, or they may want to combine small or large families with a career or intermittent work. Differences in preference may be a function of the kinds of opportunities women are exposed to outside the home. Some jobs are intrinsically more satisfying than others and offer greater opportunities for advancement; moreover, particular jobs may be more appealing to some women than to others. Accordingly, women may regard some jobs as substitutes for the rewards of motherhood, and others, not.

The kind of social approval women receive during their early adult years when they are experimenting with options to early motherhood may greatly influence the level of satisfaction derived from such options. But we must remember that women help to formulate social attitudes and that success in experimentation may provide the kind of feedback that leads to greater social acceptance of alternative life styles. Rather than there being an absence of norms, as some might fear, there would be an increase in "appropriate" options.

A diversity in life styles would undoubtedly lead to a diversity in family-size desires. This would represent a reversal in the trend over past decades toward greater uniformity in family size. In the past, as fertility declined, women increasingly wanted—and had—from two to four children. With perfect fertility control and the increase in options for women, we could expect an increase in the proportion of women who will want no children or only one child. Having several children would no longer be the primary source of self-esteem for women, and only women—and men—who truly want children would be parents. The reduction in family size would mean that motherhood would be less demanding. But it will be the increase in the proportion of women without children—at least when they are in their early twenties—that will be most significant. This will mean an increase in exposure to women who participate exclusively in nonmaternal roles. If their achievement is relatively high, an increase in such role models may enhance the aspirations of other women to achieve outside the family.

Changes in the aspirations of women, however, would not be as smooth as this suggests. As Keller (1973) has noted, women who have been socialized from infancy for marriage and motherhood may experience considerable confusion about their personal identity if these roles are challenged:

> More and more superfluous in their traditional domains and not yet fully accepted in new settings, they are caught between two incongruous worlds, the one changing too quickly, the other not quickly enough (Keller, 1973).

Accordingly, we would expect that any de-emphasis of the roles of wife and mother would initially be resisted by many women, but this would become less true over time.

IMPLICATIONS FOR THE FAMILY

If alternative life styles are pursued and women become less preoccupied with childbearing and childrearing, what will happen to the family? Will widespread participation in nonfamilial roles provide women with substitute sources of satisfaction and eliminate the need for a family?

If we consider the fact that men have been exposed to nonfamilial roles (and at higher levels of achievement than women) and still wish to marry and have children, the answer is obvious: the family will survive for some time to come because it fulfills certain needs that cannot—in our present society, at least—be filled elsewhere. Presently, women's needs may be different from men's, but both share what Dixon (1970) has termed "the pervasive need for closeness." It is not easy to break away from this dependency. Sustained intimacy has many rewards, and the family provides multiple sources: a spouse, children, and other relatives. At least for some period in their lives, most men and women will continue to seek familial sources of satisfaction.

There is no intrinsic inconsistency for women to have a family and work outside the home. As Keller (1971) has pointed out, we must consider that in other societies where most women work outside the home (Israel, Sweden, the socialist countries, and some African societies), the family has survived.

But although the family will undoubtedly survive for some time in something like its present form, what may change are the obligations of men within the family. As women become more involved outside the home, men will be pressured to become more involved inside it. There is a long way to go before responsibility will be shared equally by husbands and wives both inside and outside the home. At present, most women who work outside the home, as men do, assume the double burden of working inside the home, as men do not. This situation can be remedied to some extent by having men assume greater responsibilities in the home. We can expect that men will increasingly do this, so long as it does not threaten their nonfamilial roles. For example, we would not expect most men to readily assume child-care responsibilities while their wives work. (This lack of help is why women are currently demanding child-care facilities outside the home.) But we can expect that most men will eventually share more of the routine household chores. It may be increasingly difficult to hire domestic help—especially if opportunities for women in the work force improve—so the only alternative may be more relaxed standards in the performance of domestic chores.

Aside from the redistribution of familial obligations between husband and wife, the diversity of life styles and family-size desires may lead both men and women to postpone marriage. As noted previously, the planning of all first births would eliminate many unplanned marriages that were precipitated by a premarital conception. Since such marriages are associated with high rates of divorce (Christensen & Meissner, 1953), the planning of all first births could lead to greater marital stability. We previously noted a trend toward a slightly later age at marriage. This is true for men as well as for women. And just as the increase in child-free time permits women to experiment with alternative life styles, so too does the increase in "spouse-free" time. The growing acceptance of premarital and postdivorce sex and the ability to control fertility effectively may lead unmarried couples increasingly to experiment with alternative living arrangements, including communal living. In planning whether to have children and when, they may seriously begin to question the meaning of children in their lives. Dixon (1970) describes the diversity of options that may ensue as follows:

> Instead of living in a society where three out of four women get married between the ages of 18 and 23 and in which 19 in 20 have married

by the time they reach 40, we could look forward to a society in which some marry young, others marry in their thirties or forties or choose not to marry at all. Instead of concentrating our childbearing in the mid-twenties and producing the socially appropriate three or four children, more women could remain childless, more could have just one, and the rest could spread out according to individual temperment. We could even begin to share each other's children. Instead of having to search out our own small burrows each with its mother and father and babies, some could choose such a private world freely and others choose larger and more fluid "families" of men and women and children, or of single friends or whatever (Dixon, 1970, p. 92).

In addition to there being a difference in life styles between individuals, many men and women may come to prefer a diversity of life styles, changing over time. Some people in their twenties, for example, may prefer to be single and participate in communal living; when they are in their thirties and forties, they may prefer to be married and live in a single household—with or without children; their preference may change again to communal living as they approach old age.

CONCLUSION AND IMPLICATIONS

It may be concluded, then, that if perfect fertility control were practiced in the United States today, the impact on the roles of women would be substantial. Young women would benefit by having the experience of perfectly planning all births, including the first. Older women, who may not have planned all their births in the past, would be assured that they would not have any unplanned births in the future. The planning of births would have a greater impact on the roles of women than the reduction in family size. The predicted result would be greater diversity in family size and life styles. The family in something like its present form would continue to survive, although we might expect a further postponement of marriage and an increase in nonmarriage.

This analysis has been based on the hypothetical assumption of perfect fertility control in the United States. We cannot expect this to become a reality in the near future. However, the recent Supreme Court ruling on abortion promises to accelerate the realization of this state. The principal restraint is the problem of perfect fertility control prior to the first birth. Changes in the roles of women and the family would be greatest if this objective were achieved, but such achievement requires that contraception and induced abortion be available and practiced efficiently by all who are sexually experienced —including unmarried teenagers. Illegitimacy rates for this population have been on the rise, despite the general increase among American couples in the practice of highly effective contraceptive methods. Not only are there structural barriers that restrict the availability of effective birth control methods to unmarried teenagers, but many are not sufficiently motivated to practice contraception effectively. We have many problems to solve with regard to motivation before we can expect to achieve perfect fertility control within our society, so it will be some time before we shall witness any large-scale, dramatic changes in the roles of women or in family life.

REFERENCES

Christensen, H. T., & Meissner, H. H. 1953. "Studies in Child Spacing: Premarital Pregnancy as a Factor in Divorce." In *American Sociological Review*, Vol. 18 (1953), pp. 641–644.

Commission on Population Growth and the American Future. 1972. *Population and the American Future: Report of the Commission.* New York: New American Library.

Dixon, Ruth B. 1970. "Hallelujah the Pill?" In *Transaction,* Vol. 8 (1970), pp. 44–49, 92.

Ferriss, Abbott L. 1971. *Indicators of Trends in the Status of American Women.* New York: Russell Sage Foundation.

Keller, Suzanne. 1971. "Does the Family Have a Future?" In *Journal of Comparative Family Studies,* Spring 1971, pp. 1–14.

———. 1973. "The Future Status of Women." In *Demographic and Social Aspects of Population Growth,* Charles F. Westoff & Robert Parke, Jr., eds. Research Reports of the Commission on Population Growth and the American Future, Vol. 1. Washington: U.S. Government Printing Office.

Presser, Harriet B. 1971. "The Timing of the First Birth, Female Roles, and Black Fertility." In *Milbank Memorial Fund Quarterly,* Vol. 49 (1971), pp. 329–361.

Ridley, Jeanne Clare. 1973. "On the Consequences of Demographic Change for the Roles and Status of Women." In *Demographic and Social Aspects of Population Growth,* Charles F. Westoff & Robert Parke, Jr., eds. Research Reports of the Commission on Population Growth and the American Future, Vol. 1. Washington: U.S. Government Printing Office.

U.S. Department of Commerce, Bureau of the Census. 1961. *Census of the Population: 1960. Employment Status and Work Experience,* Series PC, no. 2. Washington: U.S. Government Printing Office.

———. 1969. *Statistical Abstract of the United States.* Washington: U.S. Government Printing Office

————. 1971a. *Marital Status and Living Arrangements: March 1971,* Series P-20, no. 225. Washington: U.S. Government Printing Office.

————. 1971b. *Fertility Indicators: 1970,* Series P-23, no. 36. Washington: U.S. Government Printing Office.

————. 1971c. *Previous and Prospective Fertility: 1967,* Series P-20, no. 211. Washington: U.S. Government Printing Office.

————. 1972. *Birth Expectations Data: June 1971,* Series P-20, no. 232. Washington: U.S. Government Printing Office.

U.S. DEPARTMENT OF HEALTH, EDUCATION AND WELFARE, CENTER FOR HEALTH STATISTICS. 1968. *Trends in Illegitimacy, United States: 1940–1965,* Series 21 (November 15, 1968). Washington: U.S. Government Printing Office.

U.S. DEPARTMENT OF HEALTH, EDUCATION AND WELFARE, PUBLIC HEALTH SERVICE. 1971. Vital Statistics of the U.S., 1968, Vol. 1: *Natality.* Washington: U.S. Government Printing Office.

U.S. DEPARTMENT OF LABOR. 1970. *Manpower Report to the President.* Washington: U.S. Government Printing Office.

WESTOFF, CHARLES F. 1972. "The Modernization of U.S. Contraceptive Practice." In *Family Planning Perspectives,* Vol. 4 (1972), pp. 9–12.

BERNARD BERELSON ══════════════════════════════

13. Population Growth Policy in Developed Countries

In recent years the "population problem" has become a well-known phenomenon. What is not so well known is that population problems have been recognized not only in the developing countries, but in the developed ones as well. For the most part, the "population problem" has been identified with traditional, agrarian, poor countries like India. But now there is concern and attention in modern, industrial, rich countries like the United States too. The "problems" are not the same, but they are there.

This is a report on population policy in 15 developed countries: Argentina, Australia, Belgium, Bulgaria, Denmark, France, Great Britain, Greece, Hungary, Israel, Japan, the Netherlands, Poland, Rumania, and the United States. By "population policy" I mean government actions that are intended to affect demographic events—population size, growth, and structure; internal distribution and international migration—or that actually do affect them, or are perceived to do so, without intent. The report, based on papers prepared by local scholars in each country, is limited to domestic population policy, although several of the countries have government programs to assist developing

Bernard Berelson is president of the Population Council in New York. His particular interest has been the application of social science to contemporary policy issues. He has worked in many fields besides population, including mass communications, political behavior, and graduate education.

nations in this field.* This summary is further limited to population growth policy, excluding problems of distribution and migration.

Taken together, these countries have a total population of about 575 million and they illustrate the major demographic and economic measures of the developed world: large and small countries, a wide range in density, low growth rates, some of the lowest birth and death rates in the world, high urbanization, high education, and high per capita incomes (see Table 13-1). Economically, educationally, and demographically, all are among the more favored nations.

BASES OF CONCERN

In the developing countries, causes for concern over population policy are reasonably clear: rapid population growth undermines economic, health, and educational development. The objective is to lower the birthrate. But what are the bases of concern in these developed countries? Of course, local circumstances vary a great deal, but in a somewhat simplified way the causes of concern can be characterized as follows.

Let us first consider national policy on the central demographic variable of mortality. All these countries have major public health programs designed to lower mortality and morbidity to the practical minimum, within the limitations of available economic and medical-technological resources. Thus a death rate "as low as possible" is typically assumed to be national policy, although that does not mean that health policy is rationally allocated accordingly. The death rates in these countries are markedly low for relatively older populations, and the female life expectancy is typically in the early- to mid-70s, or about 20 years higher than in the poor countries. However, some mortality differences by socioeconomic status undoubtedly remain in many of these countries and the distribution of health services is by no means perfect. But, to sound a theme that is common throughout this review, the policies of mortality reduction are primarily considered on grounds other than demographic considerations—in this case, on medical, economic, social, and ideological grounds.

In a few countries, there is some concern with the differences in demographic performance of ethnic groups within the community, particularly with regard to fertility. Perhaps the chief example is Israel, with essentially three demographic subcommunities, but the Flemish/

---

* A complete report, including about 25 country papers and an expanded overview, will be published in late 1973.

TABLE 13-1. COUNTRY DEMOGRAPHIC CHARACTERISTICS

Country	Population in Millions (1971 Estimate)	Density (Population per Sq. Km.) (1970)	Rate of Natural Increase (1970 or 1971)	Rate per 1,000 Population (1970 or 1971)		Percent of Population Urban	Percent of Women in Labor Force	Per Capita GDP (1970) (in U.S. $)
				Births	Deaths			
United States	207	22	0.8%	17.3	9.3	74%c	43%e	$4,734
Japan	105	280	1.3	19.2	6.6	68	uf	$1,911
Great Britain	56	240	0.5	16.2	11.6	78	37	$2,128
France	51	93	0.6	17.1	10.7	70	28	$2,901
Poland	33	105	0.9	16.8	8.2	52	39e	uf
Argentina	24	9	1.3	21.7	9.5	74	23e	$1,053
Rumania	20	85	1.2	21.1	9.5	41	48	uf
Netherlands	13	319	1.0	18.8	8.4	78	16e	$2,353
Australia	13	2	1.3	21.7	8.7	83	uf	$2,916
Hungary	10	111	0.3	14.5	11.9	44	69e	uf
Belgium	10	317	0.2	14.5	12.2	66	24	$2,633
Greece	9	67	0.8	16.5	8.4	43	uf	$1,053
Bulgaria	9	77	0.7	16.3	9.1	51	46	uf
Denmark	5	114	0.5	15.2	9.9	46	30e	$3,141
Israel	3	140	2.0	27.0	7.0	82	20	$1,836
World	3,706	27	2.0	33b	13b	33d	uf	$ 998g
Developing World	2,617a	34	2.5	40b	15b	21d	uf	$ 231g

Sources: Columns 1, 3, 4, and 5: U.N. Population and Vital Statistics Report, Statistical Papers Series A, Vol. 24, no. 3 (1 July 1972); Columns 2 and 6: U.N. Demographic Yearbook 1970, Tables 1, 2, and 5; Column 7: Ibid., Table 12 (The proportions are recent estimates [since 1965] and the denominator is the total adult female population); Column 8: U.N. Statistical Yearbook 1971.

aEstimate derived from data in source.   bU.N. Population Division, Working Paper No. 37 (17 December 1970).   cU.S. Census Bureau, 1970 Census of Population, PC(1)–A1, Table 7.   dU.N. Working Paper 44, 9 March 1972.   eFrom country reports.   fu = unavailable.   gPopulation Council, Reports on Population/Family Planning, Population and Family Planning: A Factbook, September 1972, Table 2.

Walloon differences in Belgium and the white/black differences in the United States are also relevant.

Also, a few countries (but only a few) voice concern about too much growth—that is, with the same phenomenon that causes concern in the developing countries. The reasons, however, are different and are mainly related to the potential effect on the environment of indefinitely continued population growth. This point of view is best represented among these countries by the Netherlands, where density is a special concern, and by the United States and Great Britain, where there has been a certain amount of public debate in recent years on the relationship of population to ecological or environmental problems.* Roughly speaking, these are the developed countries where the concern has been largely to reduce fertility—even though all now have rates of natural increase at or below 1 percent a year.

In more countries, the concern is to promote fertility. In Japan, earlier pressures for population growth are again being felt, now largely for economic or employment reasons. In Israel, there are political considerations in a hostile regional setting with religio-ethnic overtones and differential fertility among the key social groups is a profoundly complicating factor. In Argentina, the progrowth tendencies have political bases vis-à-vis both neighbors and the United States and tend to unite opposing political factions. In France, there has been a long history of efforts to stimulate fertility for political-ideological reasons attached to national glory. And in the Eastern European countries there is an effort to move the birthrate up for both economic and ideological reasons.

So, while most of the developing world is after lower growth and while worldwide discussion of the population problem continues to focus on that theme, the majority of these developed countries are seeking to move the other way—not far, to be sure, but still in a slightly pronatalist direction. Thus it appears that nations in particularly sensitive political positions, such as Israel, France, and Argentina, and nations with fertility near or below replacement, such as Japan, Greece, Hungary, Bulgaria, Poland, and Rumania, are not comfortable in those situations and seek remedies against demographic decline.

Not that any of these countries is really facing that. None is likely to decline in population size in the foreseeable future, short of a nuclear catastrophe. The median country on this list, with constant fer-

---

* Among these countries, the environmental issue related to population has arisen mainly in four highly industrialized countries—the United States, Great Britain, Japan, and Australia. If this issue has stamina, it probably lies ahead for other countries moving into major industrialization—and eventually, for the entire world.

tility at 1965–1970 levels, will be about 25 percent larger in the year 2000 and nearly 50 percent larger in 2020. As for zero growth in 2000 in these demographically favored nations, that would require on the average over a 25 percent linear decline in birthrates over the next three decades, which would then result in only about a 12 percent increase in population. So zero growth still seems some distance away for almost all of these countries (migration aside).

Related to the progrowth theme is the concern over immigration, either for the purpose of general development (as historically in Australia, Israel, and the United States) or for the narrower end of selective employment (as, for example, now in France, Belgium, and the Netherlands). In only a few countries is immigration still a major source of population growth—Australia and Israel are perhaps the key examples—and almost everywhere it has had ethnic reverberations (for example, the West Indians in England, the Asians in Australia, the Oriental Jews in Israel, the North Africans in France, the Southern Europeans in Western Europe, and various groups in the United States).

Finally, there is concern with the internal distribution of population or, more particularly, with the issues raised by rural to urban mobility and the resulting urban concentrations. This theme is a prominent consideration in countries where, say, more than 70 percent of the population live in urban centers, such as Australia, Britain, the Netherlands, and the United States, or with sharply growing metropolitan centers of great size, such as Buenos Aires in Argentina.

In summary, these countries are concerned with population policy for a variety of reasons: in order to move toward population stabilization for environmental and "quality of life" reasons; in order to increase the birthrate slightly for political, economic, and psychological reasons; in order to adjust the contribution of immigration to demographic growth and social differentials; and in order to effect a presumably better distribution of population within the country. All are dedicated not only to mortality control, but also to the rationale of social welfare as the end goal. And population policy is much more likely to surface as social policy of one kind or another than in its own right—as social welfare rather than as demographic causes and consequences, as one variable within overall social policy.

COURSES OF ACTION

Given this definition of the demographic situation, what actions have these countries taken with regard to both growth and distribution?

TABLE 13-2. NATIONAL AND OFFICIAL GROUPS ON POPULATION POLICY

Country	Dates	Title	Composition	Selected Mandates
Israel	1962-1966	Committee for Natality Problems	Mainly government officers	To inquire and advise the government on matters concerning natality policies, and, in particular, to consider means by which large and deprived families could be assisted.
	1968-	Demographic Center (in Office of Prime Minister)	Core staff, with public committee and executive council	"To act systematically in carrying out a natality policy intended to create a psychologically favorable climate, such that natality will be encouraged and stimulated, an increase in natality In Israel being crucial for the whole future of the Jewish people."
Greece	1968-?	Ad Hoc Committee on Demographic Policy		To study the nature, the dimensions, and the probable causes of the Greek population and to propose ethically, socially, and economically acceptable corrective measures.
Japan	1969-1971	Population Problems Advisory Council	Mainly government officers and demographic experts	
Great Britain	1970-1971	Subcommittee of Select Committee on Science and Technology	Committee of Parliament	To inquire into the consequences of population growth.
	1971-1972	Panel of experts	Outside and inside government	To assess available evidence about the significance of population trends.
United States	1970-1972	Commission on Population Growth and the American Future	Congressional and public members	To inquire into the most probable course of population growth and Internal migration to the year 2000 and the indicated impact upon governmental, economic, and environmental resources, and to assess "the various means appropriate to the ethical values and principles of this society by which our nation can achieve a population level properly suited for its environmental, natural resources, and other needs."
Hungary	1970-	Commission for Long-Range Planning of Labor Force and Standard of Living		

TABLE 13–2 (cont.)

Country	Dates	Title	Composition	Selected Mandates
Australia	1970-1973	Commission on Australia's Population and the Future	Assignment by government to Australian National University; staffed by specialists with Advisory Council	To inquire into all aspects of population in Australia: the study of the situation in countries with which Australia has particularly close associations, the study of contemporary population theories, the examination of the national growth potential, the effect of variations in rate and pattern of that growth, the distribution of population with particular reference to the growth of major urban centers and the impact of technological advance on the use of available resources.
France	1970-	High Committee on Population	Ministry of Labor, Work, and Population	To advise on matters referred by the host Ministry.
	1971-	Committee on Women's Work		
	1971-	High Consultative Committee on the Family	Ministry of Health and Social Security	
	1971-	High Medical Committee on Health		
Bulgaria	1971-	Council Dealing with Population Reproduction (of the Council of State)	Government officers	
Rumania	1971-	National Commission of Demography (of the Council of State)	Government officers, demographic experts, representatives of academies and associations	"To study the demographic phenomena, to draw up proposals . . . with regard to matters concerned with the demographic policy of the party and the State"—the evolution of demographic phenomena and processes; the effect of social and economic changes; the prospective dynamics of population and their effects on education, manpower, consumer goods, etc.; urbanization processes; preparation of policy proposals and follow-up on implementation.
Netherlands	1971-	Commission for the Study of Population Problems (the Muntendam Commission)	Government officers, scientific experts (medical, demographic, and sociological) and representatives of women's organizations	To analyze the development, density, and composition of population and its influencing factors; to study the relations between demographic development and public health; to review the rate of immigration and its social effects.

To begin with, in very recent years most of these countries have given explicit attention to their demographic situation by appointing an official commission to study and advise on population policy (see Table 13-2). Several of the countries have been concerned about population in the past—the United States in the 1930s, Japan from the early 1920s on, France throughout the century, Israel since its founding and before, Great Britain in the 1940s, Poland after World War II, and Australia every few decades in this century. But the current interest represents the most widespread official attention to population affairs since the Depression of the 1930s and perhaps the most concerted attention ever. The commissions have differing mandates, composition, duration, and position within the government structure, but they have in common a commitment to consider explicitly the effect of population trends upon the public welfare.

To that end, a number of policies affecting population have been proposed or followed in these countries.

POPULATION GROWTH

Control of Fertility

These countries have no comprehensive legal inhibitions against the practice of modern contraception, although (1) the removal of restrictive laws is only partial in France and recent in the Netherlands; (2) the opportunity is only partial in some countries because there are still medical restrictions against certain means, such as the pill in Japan; (3) the practice is not included in the public health services in a few countries, such as Israel; and (4) advertising, import, and sale of contraceptive supplies is not completely free in several countries, such as Argentina, Belgium, France, Greece, the Netherlands, and the United States.

As for induced abortion, the countries include examples of both permissive and restrictive legal policies—permissive in Japan, Hungary, Bulgaria, Poland, Denmark, Great Britain and now the United States; essentially restrictive in Belgium, Rumania, France, Israel, Greece, and Argentina; in Australia in different states; and presumably liberalizing in the Netherlands. Induced abortion is typically legalized on nondemographic grounds, usually for health reasons, but it has enough (perceived) demographic effect to be withdrawn or limited on demographic grounds, as it was recently in Rumania and as is under discussion in Japan. By all accounts, induced abortion is still an important means of fertility control in several countries where legal prohibitions are not normally enforced, such as Belgium, France, Greece, and Israel. Moreover, the situation with regard to induced abortion appears to be changing rapidly in both directions.

Thus even in these developed countries, the principle of voluntary fertility control based on modern technology, though often supported in principle, is not fully realized. It may be more nearly approximated for couples who want children, but even there the technologically possible assistance on infertility and subfecundity is probably not universally available in practice. For couples who do not want children, the technologically possible service appears to be even less available. Only in Bulgaria, Denmark, Great Britain, Hungary, and two or three states in the United States is modern fertility control widely available and practiced in a full array of technically and medically available means (see Table 13-3).

Provision of Family Assistance

Some system of family assistance or protection of the family is characteristic of these countries. It is normally justified on social welfare grounds, but often has a demographic intent as well. The system takes various forms and ranges in substance from rather small benefits to quite significant ones (see Table 13-4). Particularly noteworthy are the sharp increases in allowances for later-born children in some countries and the realistic focus in Bulgaria on the third child (a similar measure is now under consideration in Hungary). Nonetheless, it is difficult, perhaps impossible, to attribute fertility behavior directly to such allowance programs. What can be said is that countries with the lowest birthrates in the world also have, and have had for some years, some of the largest programs of family assistance tied to numbers of children.

Encouragement of Female Participation in the Labor Force

In most of these countries, women have a substantial place in the labor force and in several that place is specifically encouraged by government policy—either through various benefits provided for working women, particularly with regard to maternity and childrearing (as in the detailed provisions of the Eastern European countries, including some child-care benefits) or through laws and regulations forbidding discrimination in employment by sex (for example, the United States, culminating in the proposed Equal Rights Amendment to the Constitution). There is a correlation between fertility and women's employ-

TABLE 13-3. LEGAL POLICIES ON FERTILITY CONTROL SERVICES

Country	Legal availability of modern contraception (oral pill, IUD, condom, sterilization)	Legal availability of induced abortion	Legal fertility control services provided in government public health programs	Legal limitations on advertising, publicity, propaganda, etc., on fertility control practices
Argentina	yes, except for sterilization	no		yes
Australia	yes	one state only		
Belgium	yes	no	yes	yes
Bulgaria	yes	yes, with conditions	yes	
Denmark	yes	yes, with conditions	yes	no
France	yes, largely	no	no	yes
Great Britain	yes	yes, with conditions	yes yes	
Greece	IUD limited, no vasectomy	no		yes
Hungary	yes, but IUD recent	yes	yes	
Israel	yes	no	no	
Japan	pill and IUD no, but used	yes	yes	no
Netherlands	yes	moving in this direction		yes
Poland	yes, largely	yes, with conditions	yes	no
Rumania	yes	no, with conditions		
United States	yes	recently legally permitted	yes, generally	yes, in many states

ment (for money, outside the home), but it is a complicated one and the interrelationships are not yet altogether clear.

Manipulation of International Migration

Opening and closing this particular valve on population growth is not only available to governments; it is also sanctioned by public opinion and historical experience as a legitimate, even though coercive, means of affecting population growth, and it can be effective. Broadly, there are four positions. In some countries, international migration is a negligible factor in growth (Argentina, Japan, Denmark, Bulgaria, Hungary, Poland, and Rumania). In a few countries emigration is larger than immigration and thus exerts a negative effect on overall growth (Britain, Greece, and the Netherlands), although much of the emigration in the latter two countries is temporary rather than permanent. Third, in some countries of Western Europe (France, Belgium, the Netherlands, and Britain), short-term migration has been used to supplement the labor force, typically at the bottom. Despite its economic utility and its valued controllability, such immigration has often given rise to a range of internal problems of an ethnic character: race relations in Britain, housing and living standards of North Africans in France, and property rights in the Netherlands. In consequence, governments have been drawn further into social legislation to accommodate the situation, which in any case makes a relatively small contribution to population growth. In view of demographic pressures in the United States, the recent commission recommended no further increase in legal immigration (already by far the largest net influx in the world) and urged a halt to presumably large-scale illegal immigration. Moreover, the commission suggested that the flow of migrants be continuously monitored on demographic grounds, thus bringing the population situation into the consideration of migration for the first time. Finally, in a few countries—notably Israel and Australia, where it has contributed nearly 50 percent to recent growth—immigration has been deliberately encouraged as the most readily attainable population growth measure.

In general, the lower the growth rate, the more important immigration becomes as a demographic safety valve (as, for example, in the United States and Great Britain). The relative availability in Western Europe of a cheap labor supply from outside the country (from Southern Europe, North Africa, and the Middle East) may very well lead to a less acute national concern with a declining birthrate than that of a country like Japan.

TABLE 13-4. FAMILY ASSISTANCE PROGRAMS

Country	Marriage Payment	Birth Payment	Maternity Benefits	Maternity Leave	Children's Allowances	Tax Benefits for Families with Children
Argentina	$100	$80			for large families	yes
Australia					after first and higher for third and later children; about $1.50 per week; only small part of family income	
Belgium		$235 down to $88	free delivery (normally)	12 weeks, with reduced salary	from $16 per month to $48 per month; each child by age and number	for all low-income families
Bulgaria		*first:* 1/6 of av. monthly salary; *second:* 1.5 times av. monthly salary; *third:* 4 times av. monthly salary; *fourth and later:* 1/6 of av. monthly salary	free delivery	120 days for first child, up to 180 for third	from small increment for first child to 16% and 44% of av. monthly salary for second and third; housing and price preferences for larger families	yes, but small
Denmark					$8 per month	
France		$160	free delivery		$18 per month for 2 children, $50 for 3, up to $135 for 6	yes
Greece					$17 per month for third and later children (approximately 17% of av. monthly income	

TABLE 13-4 (cont.)

Hungary		$40 for layette	yes, incl. $40-65	20 weeks	nothing for 1, $25 per month for 2, up to $140 for 6; child-care & housing preferences for larger families	
Israel					yes, but only 2-3% of income	
Japan	no	no			below certain income, for third and later children ($10 per month)	
Netherlands				12 weeks	$12 to $35 per month per child, increasing with birth order	yes, for low-income families
Poland	yes	yes	yes	yes	recent increase of 40% for larger families	yes
Rumania	no	$190 for third and later children	free delivery	112 days with higher payment for third and later births		yes
United States	no	no	only for the poor	generally no, variable	only for the poor, as welfare payments	yes, but slight

Exhortation

This is another means by which a few governments have sought to affect population growth. Sometimes it takes the form of prizes and awards: monetary awards in Hungary and formerly in Israel for mothers of large families, medals in Bulgaria, and titles in Rumania ("Heroine Mother," "Maternal Glory"). Sometimes it is a direct call to patriotism, as with an Israeli leader's reference to one's "demographic duty" to increase the birthrate, or a proposed propaganda campaign "that the child is a great value for the Hungarian society and families taking upon themselves to bring up many children deserve the respect of the society," or a similar effort in Bulgaria. There is no evidence as to the effectiveness of such exhortation in either direction.

OBSERVATIONS

The following are some summary points that emerge from this survey of population policy in a number of developed countries:

1. Almost all the countries have become explicitly concerned with the population problem in recent years, as indicated by the appointment of official population study groups. Historically, the trend is toward explicit attention to population matters.

2. The issue continues to be sensitive, not only on religious grounds (Poland, Argentina, Greece, and the United States), but also on political and ethnic grounds—political with respect to international position (Israel, France, Australia, and Argentina), ethnic where internal divisions are related to fertility and mortality differences (Israel, the United States, France, Belgium, and Great Britain). Indeed, the rich vs. poor differences seem relatively unimportant unless attached to ethnic differences. However, the debate does continue on economic grounds, largely having to do with employment problems (vis-à-vis immigrants, for example) and it has recently branched out to environmental matters in heavily industrialized nations. The issues of population, in dispute virtually everywhere, are not conducive to an easy unanimity—they touch too many deep feelings.

3. The criteria by which demographic trends are evaluated are not solely demographic in character, but more broadly social, economic, environmental, political, and humanitarian—the protection of the family, employment needs, environmental pressures, national power, and ethical access to fertility control. That is, the roots of concern and the measures proposed are not demographic as such. It is the

way the public perceives the consequences of demographic trends for the public welfare that matters—more social policy than population policy. Accordingly, there appears to be a shift toward qualitative considerations and away from merely quantitative.

4. Partly in consequence, there remain what appear to be contradictions and conflicts in the positions of some countries. Policies, that is, often appear to lead in different directions, as when pronatalist allowances are coupled with liberal abortion policies. This is testimony to the pervasive and complicated nature of the subject and the priority of other social issues—perhaps not contradictions so much as the pursuit of different goals. Population does not rank at the top of the agenda of national problems and it seems unlikely that population problems would gain enough priority in these countries over the next years to produce a fully consistent position based exclusively on demographic considerations.

5. The major issues and their treatment appear to be quite similar among countries of different politico-economic organization—roughly speaking, capitalist and socialist. That is, the demographic conditions and the response—urban growth, environmental pressures, fertility control and abortion, female employment, family assistance, and so on—do not seem markedly different among political systems.

6. In all the effort to affect population growth, it would appear that the two most effective short-term measures have been the manipulation of immigration and of legalized abortion—in both directions. Among the measures to affect population distribution, none has worked very well in countering the movement to the metropolitan centers that characterizes all these countries. But overall, the effectiveness of policies is not very well documented, one way or the other.

7. Among this group of countries there is more concern over too little growth of population than over too much: too little in Japan, Israel, Greece, Poland, France, Bulgaria, Argentina, Hungary, Rumania, and Australia (now perhaps shifting); too much in the United States, Great Britain, and the Netherlands. Unlike the current developing world, which is, of course, in a quite different demographic position, the political interest is to sustain population growth at a low level rather than to limit growth. Countries are not at ease with too low a growth rate.

8. Although there is still not much explicit, direct population policy in these countries, the goal of population replacement as a standard component of the modernized, secularized country is dimly visible and perhaps emerging—up to replacement in a few countries, down to replacement in others. It may be that a replacement rate will become a feature of the developed world over the next decades; this

was first recommended as national policy in Japan and welcomed by the recent commission in the United States.

9. What will be the population issues over the next years in these countries? It is, of course, difficult to say with any assurance but these seem likely to be both influential and contentious over the next years —abortion, the environmental impact of population trends, urban problems, "too low" fertility, a net reproduction rate approximating replacement, and ethnic differences in fertility, mortality, and migration. Population as a social issue will continue to gain, and deserve, attention.

CHARLES F. WESTOFF ━━━━━━━━━━━━━━━━━━━━━━━━━━━

14. Recent Developments in Population Growth
Policy in the United States

A review of population policy in the United States clearly indicates that the most conspicuous recent development—in terms of both visibility and the level of government involved—was the creation in 1970 of the Commission on Population Growth and the American Future.

The commission recently released its final report—*Population and the American Future* (1972)—which includes both an analysis of the problems of population growth and distribution in the country and a series of recommendations on issues associated with population. The report is the closest this nation has come to the formulation of a national population policy. The very short history of population policy in the United States testifies to how radical a development the commission represents (Piotrow, 1973a).

THE SCOPE OF INQUIRY

Every government has enacted laws that affect population, both through direct regulation of marriage, divorce, abortion, contraception, and movement in and out of the country, and, less directly, through a variety of policies governing public health, land settlement, military service, housing, and the status of women. Most of these laws, even those closely connected with reproduction, were designed for nondemo-

This is an abbreviated version of a paper entitled "Population Policy in the U.S.," to be published in Bernard Berelson, ed., *Population Policies in Developed Countries* (New York: McGraw-Hill, 1973 [in press]).

graphic reasons and reflect the underlying sacred and secular values of the culture. Population policies in the modern sense probably have existed only when population was perceived as a problem, and even then the rationales for government action involve mainly nondemographic considerations.

Our concern here is primarily with recent official government policies that more or less directly affect population and with the attitudes and reactions of the public and various constituencies. We shall focus exclusively on questions of population growth, leaving aside in this summary, the subjects of population distribution and migration.

IMMIGRATION

The explicit "population policies" of the United States government during the nineteenth and early twentieth centuries were characteristic of a youthful nation with a seemingly ever-expanding frontier, a rapidly growing industrial economy demanding cheap labor, and a growing sense of national identity and ethnic preferences. With some exceptions, an open-door policy toward immigration had prevailed during most of the nation's history. In the 1920s restrictive legislation was enacted, following a renewed wave of immigration from Southern and Eastern Europe and the nationalistic sentiments fanned by World War I.

During the past decade, because of the sharp decline in the birthrate, the relative demographic significance of immigration has increased to the point where it currently accounts for about one-fifth of our annual growth, some 400,000 net immigrants per year. Our rate of immigration has been much greater in the past: in 1900 the immigration rate was 8 per 1000 population, while in 1970 it was only 2 per 1000. However, because of its increasing relative demographic importance, the subject of immigration has become involved in the recent population policy debate (Irwin and Warren, 1973).

There are different ways to look at the demographic role of immigration. If the U.S. population reproduced at replacement level from 1970 to the end of the century, the population would grow by some 60 million persons, one quarter of whom would be new immigrants and their descendants. From this perspective, the demographic contribution of immigration seems quite substantial. A contrary perspective is possible, however. If the fertility rate were to average slightly below replacement—2.0 rather than 2.1 births per woman—the population would eventually stabilize, even with a continuous annual flow of 400,000 net immigration. Therefore, the costs of continued immigration—assuming population stabilization to be the desirable national goal—are a slightly lower level of natural increase, a slightly later arrival at zero population growth, and a somewhat larger (8 percent) ultimate population size.

The U.S. also has a serious problem with illegal aliens, primarily in the areas near Mexico. There are estimated to be somewhere between one and two million illegal aliens in the country.

There are, of course, many nondemographic components to be considered in any discussion of immigration, including our cultural heritage, a long tradition of hospitality, foreign policy questions, economic interests, and the attitudes of minority groups. All these factors make the subject of immigration much more complex and more sensitive than if it were merely a matter of numbers.

EARLY GOVERNMENT INTEREST IN POPULATION

In the modern era, the federal government first paid explicit attention to population problems as such by creating the committee on population problems of the National Resources Committee in 1938. Opinion in some quarters held that the depressed economic conditions of the time were to some extent caused by the declining rate of population growth. Unlike today, when a stationary population and even a slowing of economic growth is increasingly perceived as desirable goals, the characteristic concern of the 1930s was with economic stagnation. Against this background and with a concern for human resources as an extension of the concept of natural resources, this committee presented its report, entitled *The Problems of a Changing Population,* to President Roosevelt in 1938. The report was commended to the consideration of government agencies, with a view to appropriate legislation and administrations, and "to the consideration of the American people in shaping broad national policies regarding our population problems."

The study committee concluded, however, that the slowing of population growth and the prospect of a stationary population should not be viewed with dismay. Although the "change from an expanding to a stabilized or slowly decreasing national population entails new economic and social problems, . . . it also opens up new possibilities of orderly progress." Indeed the committee, in its concern for the conservation of natural resources and the improvement of the standard of living, concluded that the "transition from an increasing to a stationary or decreasing population may on the whole be beneficial to the life of the nation." This conclusion bears a striking similarity to the main conclusion of the Commission on Population Growth and the American Future, which issued its report 34 years later against a totally different economic, environmental, and demographic background.

OFFICIAL VIEWS IN THE 1960s

The new interest in population matters began inauspiciously with President Eisenhower's oft-quoted statement that:

> I cannot imagine anything more emphatically a subject that is not a proper political or governmental activity. . . . This government will not . . . as long as I am here, have a positive political doctrine in its program that has to do with the problems of birth control. That's not our business.

Eisenhower's reaction only stimulated further debate. President Kennedy, after resisting U.S. birth-control aid on the grounds that such actions would be paternalistic, eventually supported U.N. population activities and acknowledged the need for research and debate. Kennedy also established a National Institute of Child Health and Human Development, which included a research program on human reproduction.

In 1965 President Johnson opened the door further in his State of the Union Message, by saying that he would "seek new ways to use our knowledge to help deal with the explosion in world population and the growing scarcity in world resources."

Several years later, funds began to grow in the Population Program of the Agency for International Development, and in 1968 President Johnson established a Committee on Population and Family Planning. This committee recommended a rapid expansion of federal family-planning programs for indigent women, acceleration of research and training programs in the biological and social sciences, government support for population studies centers, expansion of international assistance in population and family planning, and, finally, the appointment of a commission to study population (President's Committee . . . , 1968).

The most significant population legislation of the time grew partly from the Johnson Committee report and partly from President Nixon's 1969 message to Congress proposing that "we should establish as a national goal the provision of adequate family-planning services within the next five years to all those who want them but cannot afford them." In response, the 91st Congress enacted "The Family Planning Services and Population Research Act of 1970" (Public Law 91-572, S. 2108). This legislation authorized additional funds for family-planning services and for population research and established an Office of Population Affairs in the Department of Health, Education and Welfare.

THE ENVIRONMENTAL MOVEMENT

Toward the end of the 1960s, the concern about national population growth gained considerable momentum. The prime mover was, and perhaps still is, the environmental movement. This ideology captured the imagination and energies of many young people, especially students. The environmental movement centered around problems of environmental deterioration, as evidenced by air and water pollution, and the consumption of natural resources at a rate that seems to threaten their exhaustion. Many also hold the view that Americans consume a disproportionate share of the world's resources, at the expense of the rest of the world. Population growth in the U.S. is believed to multiply the problems of both pollution and resource depletion and has been indicted as one of the leading culprits in the environmental crises.

Such views were paramount in a national organization created in 1968—Zero Population Growth, Inc. (ZPG). The name reveals the goal. The high priest of this organization, and the man primarily responsible for linking the environment and population in the popular mind, is Paul Ehrlich. A professor of biology at Stanford University, Ehrlich's sensationalistic paperback book *The Population Bomb* (1968) fast became a best-seller and the gospel of the movement.

Today ZPG is an organization of some 35,000 white, middle-class, and well-educated young people, who actively campaign for legislative bills consistent with reducing population growth and promote their cause with buttons, bumper stickers, and written materials. Their early zeal for immediate zero growth and for demographic solutions to environmental problems has been tempered by a knowledge of the complexities of the situation. The leadership of the organization is now well aware of demographic realities and has become more tolerant of the lead time required to arrest the momentum of recent rapid growth.

The influence of environmental concerns is evident from data collected in the 1970 National Fertility Study. Among married women under 30 with one or two births, those concerned with population growth intend to have only about half as many additional births as those unconcerned—a relationship that is not a matter of differences in education (Rindfuss, 1973).

The debate about the role of population growth in environmental deterioration continues, although it has lost some of the dramatic sharpness of the earlier, less sophisticated arguments. There are still those who ascribe major significance to the population factor, as well as some who are unwilling to assign it any major importance. These debates have frequently pitted different professional myopias against each other. On the one hand, biologists view the problem in long-term perspective, which involves interrelationships among organisms in a sensitive, interdependent ecosystem whose delicate balances are being gravely threatened by population growth, insensitive technologies, and increasing economic growth and consumption. Economists, on the other hand, view the world in shorter time horizons and concentrate on the supply and demand for products and services, governed by a pricing system that protects against the depletion of scarce resources but that requires adjustments to charge the costs of pollution to the polluters. Proponents of this view have faith both in technological solutions to environmental problems and in the desirability of economic growth, in part as a means of providing a better standard of living for deprived people throughout the world.

As would be expected, both of these extreme views have been modified as a consequence of the debate itself and the research it has stimulated (Ridker, 1972). Concessions are visible on both sides. The biologists acknowledge the potential gains from market adjustments and technological approaches. The economists have become much more aware of the fragility of the environment and less sanguine about the ability of the economic system to correct automatically for environmental problems. And both have moderated their views on the role of population growth in the U.S., moving toward each other and toward the belief that population growth is a concern, but not a crisis.

POPULAR VIEWS

The public's views on population were also developing and changing during this period. Since 1965 several national opinion polls or sample surveys in the United States have attempted to determine the accuracy of information about population and attitudes toward population as a problem (Kantner, 1968). The most recent poll was conducted in 1971 for the Commission on Population Growth and the American Future (Lipson & Wolman, 1972). In general, the American public is now overwhelmingly in favor of the government providing birth control, is split on the question of abortion, and favors high schools offering information on ways of avoiding pregnancy. The public is quite uninformed about numbers or rates of population growth. Nonetheless, in 1971, about two-thirds regarded the growth of the U.S. population as a serious problem (up from slightly over half in 1965) and a slight majority felt that the government should try to slow down our population growth. Some two-thirds replied that they would not be concerned if U.S. population growth slowed down and gradually leveled off.

It is difficult to evaluate how much importance the public attaches to population, since most of the questions ask only about population alone. One way of assessing its relative importance on the public's agenda of problems is to compare the population problem with other leading social problems of the day. In the 1971 poll, a much higher proportion of the public felt that crime would be a greater problem than population growth over the next 30 years. Somewhat more thought pollution would be a greater problem than population. Racial discrimination and poverty were regarded almost equally as serious as population growth. More than half felt that population growth is causing the country to use up its natural resources too fast and about half felt that population growth is the main reason for air and water pollution. Only a third agreed with the statement that population growth helps keep our economy prosperous, while two-thirds felt that population growth is producing a great deal of social unrest and dissatisfaction. About three-fifths of the American public disagreed with the statement that "population growth is important in keeping up our nation's strength."

In general, the American public appears to be definitely committed to family planning and to their government's responsibility for providing the necessary programs. They know little about population, but the majority seems to feel that population is something of a problem and that slower growth would be desirable. In all probability, however, population growth is not very high on the list of national problems in the minds of most Americans.

THE BUSINESS COMMUNITY

There are two constituencies that, for different reasons, have historically supported population growth or opposed its limitation—the business community and certain conservative religious bodies, notably the Catholic Church. The traditional view of the business community has been pro-growth, although most such sentiments have been expressed as local Chamber of Commerce encouragements for increased business opportunity. In short, the belief has been simply that more people mean more customers, more workers, and more of the good life for everyone. This point of view probably still exists in many of the growing suburbs and the smaller towns and cities in certain sections of the country. But such sentiments rarely find their way into national statements. Indeed, the chief economist of the National Chamber of Commerce, in testimony presented at a public hearing of the Commission on Population Growth and the American Future—although careful to indicate that he was speaking as an individual—came out clearly for the stabilization of national population growth:

> In our society rapid population growth [while it] contributes to added effective demand and thus to increased economic growth, it intensifies existing problems of increased taxation to finance needed social investments in public facilities of education, transportation, public health, of increased urban congestion and crowding, of increased demands on and pollution of the environment. Rapid population growth thus may stimulate economic growth, but it also pre-empts much of the growth increment to be used for maintaining the existing quality of life for more people rather than improving it. . . . The U.S. population issue, viewed domestically, is whether we wish for added numbers of U.S. people to pre-empt the resources of ours and the rest of the world to meet the demands for larger quantities of facilities.

Another indication that the business community has altered its view on the subject comes from a 1970 *Fortune* magazine poll of the executives of the country's 500 leading corporations (Mayer, 1970). Some 8 out of 10 of these executives favored some sort of effort to curb further population growth. Such opinion reflects both a growing collective sense of social responsibility by business and a new perception of environmental responsibilities.

THE CATHOLIC CHURCH

Catholics constitute about one-quarter of the U.S. population. By virtue of the size of its constituency and through its organizations and hierarchy, the Catholic Church plays an important role in the nation's political life and hence in questions of population policy. In the past ten years liberalizing, if not radical, changes have occurred in the attitudes and practices of Catholics and their clergy in connection with fertility control (Burch, 1971). This fact makes it increasingly difficult to generalize about Catholics or the Church, but the Catholic Church nevertheless continues to exert a strong conservative influence on social change in the area of population policy. It should be emphasized, however, that this current conservative position, especially if we think of actual Catholic practices and attitudes, would have been regarded as quite radical by the standards of only a decade ago.

The orthodox or traditional view, still held by many, if not most, clergy (especially the bishops), is that the primary purpose of marriage is procreation. Official Church teaching on contraception was stated in the 1968 Papal Encyclical, *Humanae Vitae*, which reiterated this view and held that all methods of fertility control except the rhythm method are illicit. In 1965, before the encyclical, research had revealed that the majority of Catholic couples were using illicit methods of birth control. By 1970, after the encyclical, the proportion of Catholics using contraception other than rhythm had grown even higher.

This deviation from official teaching has been buttressed by and reflected in the growing liberal views of some clergy, who hold that companionship and affection are equally valid purposes of marriage and have to be balanced against the procreative function. Thus, contraceptive practice does not interfere with, and indeed can contribute to, the proper fulfillment of marriage. In this respect, the liberal Catholic theologians and clergy are moving toward the positions taken earlier by many Protestant and Jewish spokesmen who have incorporated a growing sense of social responsibility into traditional moral theology.

Although cracks are visible in the official Catholic position on contraception, there is no evidence that such liberalization of thought has carried over to the subject of abortion. Whereas many Protestant and Jewish religious leaders have supported the liberalization of abortion laws (although conservative wings of both groups have opposed the trend), the Catholic hierarchy has maintained unbroken ranks in opposition. In fact, some of the softening of resistance to contraception may well be a result of the closing of ranks on the abortion issue.

The most recent manifestation of the opposition to relaxation of abortion laws occurred after the Supreme Court announced its ruling, which, in effect, will leave the decision to have an abortion through the first six months of pregnancy to the woman and her doctor. Cries of moral outrage were immediately heard from leading American cardinals and from the Vatican itself.

Nonetheless, the attitudes of the Catholic population have shifted significantly in the past five years and can be expected to shift even more in the future. Currently, however, the great majority still remain opposed to unrestricted availability of abortion services. Between 1965 and 1970, the proportion of Catholic married women who endorsed the idea of abortion in case of rape increased from 43 to 63 percent; because of the possible deformity of the child, from 40 to 59 percent; in the event the woman was unmarried, from 9 to 22 percent; in case the couple could not afford another child, from 8 to 16 percent; and, if the couple simply did not want another child, from 5 to 14 percent (Jones & Westoff, 1973).

Catholic views on population growth and population policy are more diffuse and varied. The American bishops' denunciation of the report of the Commission on Population Growth and the American Future is the most conspicuous and explicit indication of the Church's attitude. It would have been interesting to observe the reaction of the Church if the commission's report had not included the abortion recommendation. But unless the report had unequivocally repudiated the liberalization of abortion laws, it is likely that it still would have been met with suspicion.

Catholic public opinion is not really crystallized as "Catholic," except when the abortion issue is involved. Otherwise Catholics are just as exposed to the environmental and social issues of the day as are other citizens. Thus on such questions as whether U.S. population growth or distribution is considered a serious problem, whether the slowing and gradual leveling off of national population growth should be a concern or not, and even on whether birth control should be made available by the federal government to all on request or on whether high schools should offer information on how to avoid pregnancy, the 1971 public opinion poll found that Catholics are generally indistinguishable from non-Catholics.

ETHNIC GROUPS

Blacks, Mexican-Americans, and other deprived minority groups in the United States attach little importance to problems of national population growth. Indeed, discussion of population policy appears increasingly to provoke indifference at best and suspicion or even hostility in some quarters. Even family planning programs have met with some resistance.

In the black community, the deepest emotional source of this attitude is apprehension that population-policy and fertility-control programs are genocidal attempts by the white to eliminate the black (Darity, 1971; Willie, 1971). Such an attitude is reinforced by the appearance in ghettoes of birth-control clinics without pediatric or maternal health clinics, or by occasional public proposals for compulsory sterilization of women on welfare who have an additional child. Another related source is the concern that the dominant white community is trying to substitute population control for economic development—an attitude not dissimilar to that voiced occasionally by representatives of some developing nations. Still another expression of this view connects increasing population with increasing political power—a view strengthened by recent elections of black mayors and other government officials.

Differences between black and white popular views of the subject, though not great, do exist. According to 1971 public opinion data, half of the black population, compared with two-thirds of the white population, regard the growth of the U.S. population as a serious problem. When asked whether they would be concerned if U.S. population growth slowed down and gradually leveled off, some 42 percent of the black population, compared with 26 percent of the white population, expressed concern. And although the great majority (77 percent) of blacks are in favor of the government making birth control available to all men and women who want it, their support for such services is somewhat lower than that of whites (88 percent). When this comparison is confined to women, however, we find no difference. To a considerable extent, in fact, ideological objections are made by men, while the black women who are more directly involved with the problems and responsibilities of unwanted births are much more receptive to family planning. Black women who have been interviewed in fertility surveys are very similar to white women in their concern about the control of fertility, although their ability to exercise effective control has until recently been handicapped by lack of information and access to effective methods. There was a 56 percent reduction in the incidence of unwanted fertility among blacks between 1961 and 1965 and 1966 and 1970, a dramatic indication that black women are acquiring the knowledge of and access to modern methods of fertility control (Ryder & Westoff, 1973). Their attitudes toward abortion have also grown increasingly permissive, although in 1970 they are still more opposed to the idea than whites (Jones & Westoff, 1973).

The picture of black attitudes is thus diverse, ranging from indifference to animosity. In the black population at large, however, the average person, especially the woman, is just as anxious to regulate her childbearing as is her white counterpart.

THE WOMEN'S LIBERATION MOVEMENT

There are two very basic similarities between the women's rights and black militant ideologies: both distrust a large segment of society and both regard the equality of social and economic opportunity as the main political objective, for which population policy and birth control are no substitutes. But there the similarity ends.

Women obviously have a special stake in the matter of birth control. Their movement has been particularly outspoken on behalf of permissive abortion laws and the right of the woman to control childbearing. This view is simply an extension of the position taken decades ago by the early feminist movement. It is now more strident and demanding and accompanied by more resentment of the fact that the male seems to escape much of the responsibility for preventing conception.

Aside from their position on women's rights with respect to childbearing, the main relevance of the women's liberation movement for population is the drive for equal economic opportunity. Legislatively this has assumed many forms, including the proposed Equal Rights Amendment and demands for child-care centers and tax deductions for the costs of child care. There is some question about how effective such antinatalist policies as day-care centers and tax deductions for child care would be, since they might have the effect of making it easier for a woman to have children *and* work. Whether exposure to alternative interests that are competitive with childbearing will outweigh the financial subsidies of childbearing is an empirical question that only time and observation can resolve.

POPULATION GROWTH POLICY

These, then, are some of the main forces influencing the development of population policy in the United States. In the summer of 1969 President Nixon, in a message to Congress, gave the impression that a national population policy might actually be in the offing. At that time he said:

> If the present rate of growth continues, the third hundred million persons will be added in roughly a 30-year period. This means that by the year 2000, or shortly thereafter, there will be more than 300 million Americans.

> This growth will produce serious challenges for our society. I believe that many of our present social problems may be related to the fact that we have had only 50 years in which to accommodate the second hundred million Americans. . . . Where, for example, will the next hundred million Americans live? . . . Are our cities prepared for such an influx? . . . Are there ways, then, of readying our cities? Alternatively, can the trend toward greater concentration of our population be reversed? . . . Are there ways of fostering a better distribution of

the growing population? . . . What of our natural resources and the quality of our environment? . . . How can we better assist American families so that they will have no more children than they wish to have? . . . Perhaps the most dangerous element in the present situation is the fact that so few people are examining these questions from the viewpoint of the whole society. . . . It is for all these reasons that I today propose the creation by Congress of a Commission on Population Growth and the American Future. . . . One of the most serious challenges to human destiny in the last third of this century will be the growth of the population. Whether man's response to that challenge will be a cause for pride or for despair in the year 2000 will depend very much on what we do today. . . . When future generations evaluate the record of our time, one of the most important factors in their judgment will be the way in which we responded to population growth.

In March of 1970 Congress created the Commission on Population Growth and the American Future and assigned it several tasks: to inquire into the most probable course of population growth, internal migration, and related demographic developments between now and the year 2000; to examine the public economic resources required to deal with anticipated population growth; to evaluate the probable impact of population growth on government activities, on natural resources, and on the environment; and, finally, to assess "the various means appropriate to the ethical values and principles of this society by which our nation can achieve a population level properly suited for its environmental, natural resources, and other needs."

After two years of research, public hearings, and deliberations, the commission issued its final report. The first part of the report was an analysis of the nature of the population issue in the United States: the impacts of growth on the economy, government services, resources, and the environment, and implications for the family, minority groups, and the aged. The second part of the report developed a series of recommendations on diverse subjects related to population: education, child care, adoption, the status of women, family planning, contraceptive research, abortion, immigration, and different aspects of population distribution. The report concluded with a series of recommendations for the improvement of population statistics, the expansion of population research, and the organization of population activities within the federal government.

The commission's basic conclusions were that the nation "can no longer afford the uncritical acceptance of the population growth ethic that 'more is better' " and "that no substantial benefits would result from continued growth of the nation's population." It reached these conclusions by examining the impact of the two- vs. the three-child family between 1970 and 2000 on various aspects of the quality of life in America. It concluded that slower population growth and the eventual stabilization of population size would raise per capita income, have no deleterious effects on business or industry, ease the pressures on resources and the environment, and permit the investment of public funds to improve the quality of education and other government services rather than to continually expand facilities. Similarly, further population growth was seen as essentially irrelevant to national security. The benefits seem overwhelming, but there may also be some costs associated with a stationary population, notably an increase in the proportion of persons aged 65 and over (from 9.8 percent in 1970 to 16 percent) and a reduction by about one-third in the proportion under 18 (from 34 to 24 percent). An older, nongrowing population might be less innovative and provide less opportunity for upward social mobility, but such possibilities are much less firmly grounded in evidence than are the numerous benefits associated with reduced growth.

The commission concluded that the nation would not benefit if population growth were to continue beyond what the past momentum of growth implies. However, it did not set zero population growth as a national goal, toward which all of its policy recommendations were aimed. In this sense, it therefore differed from the unsuccessful resolution introduced into Congress by Senator Alan Cranston of California (U.S. Senate, 1971). Instead, the commission developed recommendations that were worthwhile in themselves, while at the same time speaking to population issues. These sought to maximize information and knowledge about human reproduction and the responsibilities of parenthood, to improve the quality of the setting in which children are raised, to neutralize social and institutional pressures that historically have been pronatalist in character, and to enable couples to avoid unwanted childbearing, thereby improving their chances to realize their own fertility preferences. Although the analysis of the population question showed the advantages of slower growth for the society as a whole, the actual recommendations the commission made to the President and Congress concentrated on enhancing the freedom of individuals to have the number of children they wanted. It is, of course, true that fertility had been declining and that the elimination of unwanted childbearing would contribute significantly to the achievement of zero growth. Nevertheless, certain recommendations were offered that might just as easily increase fertility as decrease it. The stabilization of population was viewed as a welcome consequence of maximizing individual choice. No important recommendation to reduce immigration was made, other than that of illegal aliens.

It is entirely possible that implementing the commission's recommendations could drive fertility below replacement, a condition that could lead to an ultimate loss of population if it were continued. The commission recognized this possibility and observed: "We are not concerned about this latter contingency because, if sometime in the future the nation wishes to increase its population growth, there are many possible ways to try this; a nation's growth should not depend on the ignorance and misfortune of its citizenry." In fact, the commission regarded the report in part as an educational effort to dispel the anxieties about below-replacement fertility that often arise in countries on the threshhold of such low fertility.

It is too early to evaluate the basic impact of the report. Initial responses have been mixed. Newspaper editorial comment has been generally quite favorable. As indicated earlier, the response of the Catholic Church has been hostile; other religious leaders, primarily Protestant, have supported it. Although many individuals in high positions in the government have privately expressed support for the recommendations, the President's response was essentially a restatement of his personal opposition to permissive abortion laws and to providing access to contraception for teenagers. Conspicuously absent was any response to the consensus on the desirability of population stabilization or to the many recommendations in connection with population movement. The fact that the report was issued in an election year has undoubtedly contributed to the limited, narrowly political presidential reaction. But most activities in the population field have been initiated and developed by Congress rather than by the executive office of the President (Piotrow, 1973b). These possibilities notwithstanding, however, the United States does not yet have any explicit population policy.

CONCLUSIONS

We have seen that the United States does not yet have an explicit population policy, if that term includes a population growth goal. Perhaps there is no need for such a policy if the main concern is the growth rate. If very recent trends continue, U.S. fertility will be *below* replacement in the near future and it will be interesting indeed to observe public reaction.

But population policy is and should be a much broader concept than a rate of growth and the means to achieve it. It should include opportunities for couples to reproduce under optimal circumstances— a notion that includes considerations of the health of the mother and baby and a maximum of freedom of choice for the couple about marriage and the reproductive decision. There have been many developments in the U.S. in the last decade or so that have enhanced the individual's freedom to exercise better control over his or her fertility. The collective consequences of these developments has been to slow our rate of population growth considerably, which appears to imply considerable advantages to the society as a whole. Perhaps "population policies," in the explicit sense of the term, only develop when the behavior of individuals and the welfare of society are seen as markedly divergent.

REFERENCES

BURCH, THOMAS K. 1971. "Catholic Parish Priests and Birth Control: A Comparative Study of Opinion in Colombia, the United States and the Netherlands." In *Studies in Family Planning*, Vol. 2, no. 6 (June 1971), pp. 121–136.

COMMISSION ON POPULATION GROWTH AND THE AMERICAN FUTURE. 1972. *Population and the American Future: Report of the Commission*. Washington: U.S. Government Printing Office.

DARITY, WILLIAM A. 1971. "Race Consciousness and Fears of Black Genocide as Barriers to Family Planning." In *Population Reference Bulletin,* Selection No. 37 (June 1971), pp. 5–12.

ERLICH, PAUL R. 1968. *The Population Bomb*. New York: Ballantine Books.

IRWIN, RICHARD, and WARREN, ROBERT. 1973. "Demographic Aspects of American Immigration." In *Aspects of Population Growth Policy,* Robert Parke, Jr., & Charles F. Westoff, eds. Research Reports of the Commission on Population and the American Future, Vol. 6. Washington: U.S. Government Printing Office, pp. 167–78.

JONES, ELISE, & WESTOFF, CHARLES F. 1973. "Attitudes toward Abortion in the U.S. in 1970 and the Trend since 1965." In *Aspects of Population Growth Policy*, Robert Parke, Jr., & Charles F. Westoff, eds. Research Reports of the Commission on Population Growth and the American Future, Vol. 6. Washington: U.S. Government Printing Office, pp. 569–78.

KANTNER, JOHN F. 1968. "American Attitudes on Population Policy: Recent Trends." In *Studies in Family Planning*, no. 30 (May 1968), pp. 1–6.

LIPSON, GERALD, & WOLMAN, DIANNE. 1972. "Polling Americans on Birth Control and Population." In *Family Planning Perspectives*, Vol. 4, no. 1 (January 1972), pp. 39–42.

MAYER, LAWRENCE A. 1970. "U.S. Population Growth: Would Slower Be Better?" In *Fortune* (June 1970), pp. 80–83, 164–168.

NATIONAL RESOURCES COMMITTEE. 1938. *The Problems of a Changing Population*. Washington: U.S. Government Printing Office.

PIOTROW, PHYLLIS T. 1973a. *World Population Crisis: The United States Response.* New York & London: Praeger Publishers.

————. 1973b. "Congressional-Executive Relations in the Formation of Explicit Population Policy." In *Aspects of Population Growth Policy*, Robert Parke, Jr., & Charles F. Westoff, eds. Research Reports of the Commission on Population Growth and the American Future, Vol. 6. Washington: U.S. Government Printing Office.

PRESIDENT'S COMMITTEE ON POPULATION AND FAMILY PLANNING. 1968. In *Population and Family Planning.* Washington: U.S. Department of Health, Education and Welfare.

RIDKER, RONALD. 1972. "Resource and Environmental Consequences of Population Growth in the United States." In *Population, Resources, and the Environment*, Ronald Ridker, ed. Research Reports of the Commission on Population Growth and the American Future, Vol. 3. Washington: U.S. Government Printing Office.

RINDFUSS, RONALD R. 1973. "Recent Trends in Population Attitudes." In *Aspects of Population Growth Policy*, Robert Parke, Jr., & Charles F. Westoff, eds. Research Reports of the Commission on Population Growth and the American Future, Vol. 6. Washington: U.S. Government Printing Office, pp. 17–34.

RYDER, NORMAN, & WESTOFF, CHARLES F. 1973. "Wanted and Unwanted Fertility in the United States: 1965 and 1970." In *Demographic and Social Aspects of Population Growth*, Robert Parke, Jr., & Charles F. Westoff, eds. Research Reports of the Commission on Population Growth and the American Future, Vol. 1. Washington: U.S. Government Printing Office, pp. 467–87.

U.S. SENATE JOINT RESOLUTION TO DECLARE A U.S. POLICY OF ACHIEVING POPULATION STABILIZATION BY VOLUNTARY MEANS. In *Congressional Record,* Vol. 117, no. 82 (June 2, 1971).

WESTOFF, CHARLES F. 1973. "Population Policy in the United States." In *Population Policies in the Developed Countries*, Bernard Berelson, ed. New York: McGraw-Hill.

WILLIE, CHARLES V. 1971. "Perspectives from the Black Community." In *Population Reference Bulletin*, Selection No. 37 (June 1971), pp. 1–4.